Spanish AS

ánimo 1

Teacher's Book

Isabel Alonso de Sudea

Vincent Everett
María Isabel Isern Vivancos

UNIVERSITY PRESS

Great Clarendon Street, Oxford OX2 6DP

Oxford University Press is a department of the University of Oxford.
It furthers the University's objective of excellence in research, scholarship, and education by publishing worldwide in

Oxford New York

Auckland Cape Town Dar es Salaam Hong Kong Karachi
Kuala Lumpur Madrid Melbourne Mexico City Nairobi
New Delhi Shanghai Taipei Toronto

With offices in

Argentina Austria Brazil Chile Czech Republic France
Greece Guatemala Hungary Italy Japan South Korea
Poland Portugal Singapore Switzerland Thailand Turkey
Ukraine Vietnam

Oxford is a registered trade mark of Oxford University Press in
the UK and in certain other countries

British Library Cataloguing in Publication Data

Data available

ISBN 978 019 915331 2

10 9 8 7 6 5 4

Typeset by Thomson

Printed in Great Britain by Bell & Bain, Glasgow

Acknowledgements

The author and publisher would like to thank Blanca González
(language consultant), Michelle Armstrong (editor),
Virginia Masardo (editor).

Contents

Symbols used in this Teacher's Book:

 Listening material available on CD

S Self-study CD

Summary of unit contents

Ánimo and AQA Specification match

AQA topics (AS level)	Ánimo units
Media	
♦ Television: TV viewing habits; Range of programmes, e.g. their appeal and popularity; Range of channels including satellite and Internet; Benefits and dangers of watching TV	A1 Unit 1
♦ Advertising: Purposes of advertising; Advertising techniques; Curbs on advertising, e.g. tobacco, alcohol; Benefits and drawbacks of advertising	A1 Unit 1
♦ Communication techology: Popularity of mobile phones, MP3 players, etc.; Benefits and dangers of mobile phones, MP3 players, etc.; Internet – its current and potential usage; Benefits and dangers of Internet	A1 Unit 2
Popular culture	
♦ Cinema: Types of film, changing trends; The place of cinema in popular culture; A good film I have seen; Cinema versus alternative ways of viewing films	A1 Unit 3
♦ Music: Types of music, changing trends; The place of music in popular culture; Music I like; How music defines personal identity	A1 Units 2, 3
♦ Fashion/trends: How we can alter our image; Does how we look define who we are?; Lifestyle and leisure activities; The cult of celebrity	A1 Unit 4
Healthy living/lifestyle	
♦ Sport/exercise: Traditional sports versus 'fun'sports; Reasons for taking part in sport/physical exercise; Factors influencing participation in sport/physical exercise; Links between physical exercise and health	A1 Units 5, 6
♦ Health and well-being: Alcohol, tobacco, other drugs; Diet, including eating disorders; The 'work/life balance'; Risks to health through accidents	A1 Unit 6
♦ Holidays: Types of holiday and holiday activities; The impact of tourism on holiday destinations; Purposes and benefits of holidays; Changing attitudes to holidays	A1 Unit 7
Family/relationships	
♦ Relationships within the family: Role of parents and importance of good parenting; Attitudes of young people towards other family members; Conflict between young people and other family members; Changing models of family and parenting	A1 Unit 8
♦ Friendships: Characteristics and roles of friends; Conflicts with friends; Importance of friends; Friendship versus love	A1 Units 4, 8
♦ Marriage/partnerships: Changing attitudes towards marriage or cohabitation; Separation and divorce; Staying single: benefits and drawbacks; Changing roles within the home	A1 Unit 8

Ánimo and Edexcel Specification match

Edexcel topics (AS level)	Ánimo units
Media	
Youth culture and concerns	
♦ Music and fashion	A1 Units 2, 3
♦ Technology (e.g. MP3s/blogs/mobile phones/Internet/games)	A1 Unit 2
♦ Relationships (family/friendships and peer pressure)	A1 Units 4, 8
♦ Drink, drugs, sex	A1 Unit 6
Lifestyle: health and fitness	
♦ Sport and exercise	A1 Unit 5
♦ Food and diet	A1 Unit 6
♦ Health issues (e.g. smoking, skin cancer, health services)	A1 Unit 6
The world around us: travel, tourism, environmental issues and the Spanish-speaking world	
♦ Tourist information, travel and transport	A1 Puente, Unit 7
♦ Weather (e.g. natural disasters, climate change)	A1 Unit 7
♦ Pollution and recycling	A1 Unit 7
Education and employment	
♦ Education (schooling and higher education)	A1 Unit 9
♦ Educational policy and student issues	A1 Unit 9
♦ The world of work (e.g. the changing work scene, job opportunities and unemployment)	A1 Unit 9

Ánimo and WJEC Specification match

WJEC topics (AS level)	Ánimo units
Leisure and Lifestyle	
♦ Travel and tourism	A1 Unit 7
♦ Sport	A1 Unit 5
♦ Hobbies	A1 Units 2, 3
♦ Entertainment	A1 Units 1, 3
♦ Customs	A1 Units 3, 5, 6
♦ Traditions	A1 Units 5, 8
♦ Healthy living – health and nutrition, diet and exercise	A1 Units 5, 6
♦ Unhealthy living – drugs, aids, smoking, alcohol, etc.	A1 Unit 6
The Individual and Society	
♦ Relationships and responsibilities	A1 Units 4, 8
♦ Gender issues	A1 Unit 8
♦ Youth culture (values, peer groups, fashions and trends etc.)	A1 Units 2, 4, 8
♦ Education	A1 Unit 9
♦ Vocational training and future careers	A1 Unit 9

Introduction

The course

Welcome to **Ánimo 1!**

Ánimo 1 is the first stage of a two-part Spanish course written to match the new AS and A2 specifications for AQA, Edexcel, WJEC and CCEA. It has been written by a team of experienced authors and practising teachers and is suitable for a wide range of learners.

Rationale

The aims of **Ánimo 1** are:

♦ to provide thorough coverage of the AS specifications for AQA, Edexcel, WJEC and CCEA (see grids on pages 6–8 of this book) and prepare students for the AS examinations

♦ to provide material suitable for AS students of all abilities to ease the transition from GCSE to AS level

♦ to provide comprehensive grammatical coverage and practice of the QCA-defined grammatical content

♦ to help students develop specific learning strategies, for example dictionary skills, independent study, vocabulary learning and pronunciation techniques

♦ to enable students to take control of their own learning by means of learning strategies, reference and revision sections, study skills and opportunities for independent study

♦ to encourage success by providing clear objectives and by practising language via activities with a clear purpose

♦ to provide up-to-the-minute information on current affairs and language learning activities

The components of Ánimo 1

Students' Book

The Students' Book is the complete handbook for advanced level studies, providing a comprehensive and integrated programme of teaching, practice, revision and reference for students. This 176-page book contains the following sections:

Puente

This initial unit bridges the gap between GCSE and AS level by providing revision of key language and grammar and focusing on topics that should be familiar to students from their previous learning. It also introduces students to the layout of the Students' Book and the types of activity they will encounter in **Ánimo.**

Unidades 1–9

There are nine units on different topics. Each unit has been planned to be interesting and motivating, as well as to develop relevant strategies and skills for independent study and preparation for examinations. An outline of the content of each unit is given on Teacher's Book pages 4–5.

Repasos

After every two units, there are two pages with a range of revision activities, aimed at providing further practice and consolidation of the language of the preceding units. Some of the activities are suitable for use in class whereas others are more suitable for homework.

Repaso final

This section on pages 136–45 provides practice material drawn from the whole of **Ánimo 1,** including revision of key grammar points and skills. The listening, speaking, reading and writing activities on pages 136–40 can be used as practice examination material.

Gramática

This detailed reference section complements the grammar explanations given within the body of the Students' Book. All explanations are in English so that students are able to use it independently.

Vocabulario

This Spanish–English glossary contains many of the words from the Students' Book.

9

Teacher's Book

Detailed teaching notes for each unit are provided. These notes include:

♦ suggestions for using the material in the Students' Book, including the revision pages
♦ answers to most activities, including possible answers where appropriate as well as the correct answers for true/false activities
♦ transcripts for all recorded material
♦ diagnostic tests
♦ a sample scheme of work

Resource and Assessment CD-Rom

The Resource and Assessment CD-Rom provides five copymasters for each unit:

♦ three general copymasters
♦ one grammar copymaster
♦ one skills copymaster

Assessment material and planning grids are also included on the Resource and Assessment CD-Rom.

Grammar Workbook

This 96-page Workbook contains thorough revision and practice of grammar covered in the Students' Book, with an answer booklet for self-marking if appropriate.

CDs

The CDs provide the listening material to accompany the Students' Book. The scripted material was recorded by native Spanish speakers. All CDs may be copied within the purchasing institution for use by teachers and students. The **Ánimo solo** CD is ideal for self-study and it is advisable for students to have an individual copy of this CD to practise independent listening.

CD contents

CD 1:   Puente, Unidades 1–3
CD 2:   Unidades 4–8
CD 3:   Unidad 9, Repaso final

Features of an Ánimo unit

Unit objectives

Each unit begins with a list of topics with page references to their place in the unit. There are also objectives in English that provide clear information to students about what they will learn in the unit, including grammar and skills. The first two pages of each unit contain a visual stimulus and some activities to introduce the theme of the unit.

Core spreads

Each of the four core spreads begins with one or two questions to pinpoint what students will learn.

Activities in all four skills are included on each spread, leading to a productive spoken and written task at the end of the spread.

Frases clave

These boxes provide key phrases for students to use in their written and spoken outcome tasks.

Gramática

Most spreads feature a *Gramática* section, focusing on a key grammar point. The explanations and instructions in these sections are in English, enabling students to use them independently. Activities are provided (lettered A, B, C, etc.) to reinforce each grammar point, and examples are included in texts on the spread so that students have an opportunity to see the grammar point in practice. There are also cross-references to pages in the grammar reference section and the Grammar Workbook.

Técnica

These sections provide practical skills advice and language-learning tips in English, with activities (lettered A, B, C, etc.) enabling students to put the advice into practice. They are ideal for self-study and are intended to improve aspects of students' performance and help them develop as independent learners.

Extra

These are additional activities, often provided on a copymaster, to extend what students have learnt on the spread.

Gramática en acción

This page (on the final spread of each unit) provides additional activities to reinforce or extend key grammar points from the unit.

A escoger

At the end of each unit there is a page of self-study activities to reinforce the language, skills and grammar that students have learnt in the unit. The listening activities are recorded on a self-study CD.

Repasos and Repaso final

These sections provide revision practice with exam-style questions to help students prepare for their AS examination.

Ánimo and the new AS and A2 specifications

Ánimo is a structured two-part course intended for use over two years' study and has been written to follow the revised AS/A2 specifications for AQA, Edexcel, WJEC and CCEA. There are nine units in **Ánimo 1**, written to match the content of the revised AS specifications (for first teaching from 2008). The style and content of the activities would also be appropriate for use with other exam specifications.

Grammar

Ánimo 1 provides complete coverage of the QCA-defined grammar content. The deductive approach on the Students' Book pages and the extensive practice provided in the Grammar Workbook ensure that students are able to master all aspects of language structure required at this level.

Assessment

The assessment material in **Ánimo 1** has been written to match the style of the major examination boards. Practice in tackling exam-style questions is provided in the *Repasos* and *Repaso final* sections and in the assessments on the Resource & Assessment CDs. Mark schemes for the assessments are provided in the teaching notes that are included on the Resource & Assessment CDs.

Key skills

The table below provides an overview of key skills coverage in **Ánimo 1**. It shows where there are opportunities to develop and/or assess some or all of the criteria for each key skill at level 3.

The following notes provide examples of how each key skill may be developed or assessed through the activities in **Ánimo 1**:

Communication

Teachers should note that, although the study of a modern foreign language helps students to develop their communication skills, *the evidence for this Key Skill must be presented in English, Irish or Welsh*. **Ánimo 1** offers opportunities for practising and developing communication skills rather than for generating assessed evidence.

For this key skill, students need to:

1a Take part in a group discussion
All **Ánimo 1** units provide opportunities for students to discuss topics in pairs, small groups or as a whole-class activity.

1b Make a formal presentation of at least eight minutes
Many of the topics covered in the coursebook provide a suitable basis for a presentation. See also the *Técnica* section in Unit 3, which provides specific guidance on speaking from notes. Students should be encouraged to support their presentations using visuals (e.g. OHP transparencies, photographs, brochures, etc.), PowerPoint, audio clips and other appropriate material.

2 Read and synthesise information from at least two documents about the same subject
Ánimo 1 provides reading material on a wide range of topics, with activities designed to help students identify main points and summarise information. Students are also encouraged to undertake wider reading when researching information for productive spoken and written work. Their wider reading might include newspapers, magazines, books, publicity material, and Internet sources.

		Ánimo 1 units									
		Puente	1	2	3	4	5	6	7	8	9
Main key skills	Communication	✓	✓	✓	✓	✓	✓	✓	✓	✓	✓
	Application of number			✓	✓		✓		✓	✓	
	ICT	✓	✓	✓	✓	✓	✓	✓	✓	✓	✓
Wider key skills	Working with others	✓	✓	✓	✓	✓	✓	✓	✓	✓	✓
	Improving own learning and performance	✓	✓	✓	✓	✓	✓	✓	✓	✓	✓
	Problem solving	✓	✓	✓	✓	✓	✓	✓	✓	✓	✓

3 Write two different types of document
Opportunities exist throughout **Ánimo 1** for students to attempt extended writing in a variety of styles, e.g. reports, essays and creative material on a wide range of themes, a film review, a biography, publicity material, informal and formal letters, etc.

Application of number

Although it may not be within the scope of a modern foreign language course to generate sufficient evidence to assess this key skill, **Ánimo 1** does provide opportunities for students to develop their ability to work with numbers. Numbers feature in most units (e.g. dates/years, percentages, statistics, population figures, etc.); however, the table on page 8 indicates only those units where students are involved in interpreting or commenting on statistics.

Information and communications technology

Students need to be able to:
1   search for and select information
2   enter and develop the information, and derive new information
3   present combined information such as text with image, text with number, image with number

All **Ánimo 1** units provide opportunities for students to develop aspects of this key skill. Criteria 1-3 (listed above) can be combined in a single extended piece of work in activities such as the following:

♦   Unit 4, page 67, activity 2b: Students read a text about the effects of computer games and use their ideas to design a leaflet giving information about their advantages and disadvantages. This could be produced using desktop publishing.

♦   Unit 7, page 99, activity 5: Students use the Internet to find out about a Latin American country of their choice. They then use this information to produce an advert which aims to attract tourists to this country.

Working with others

All **Ánimo 1** units provide opportunities for students to work together, either in a one-to-one situation or as part of a group. These opportunities may take the form of interviews, discussions, debates and surveys, or they may involve students in a more creative activity such as producing an advertisement or a PowerPoint presentation, or inventing a role-play.

The following example shows how a group task can be developed and expanded in order to become a suitable means of assessing this key skill:

Unit 2, page 31, activity 3: Students work in groups to prepare a presentation to advertise one of the items on page 30.

1   They begin by agreeing on which of the technological items they wish to promote and choosing a name for it. What market should they aim the advertising at? What name would best suit that market? How could the product best be advertised?

2   Once they have allocated roles and responsibilities within the group, students then work towards creating promotional material for their chosen piece of technology, checking regularly on progress and dealing with problems as they occur. Then students present their piece of advertising to the rest of the class.

3   Finally, the whole class vote on which piece of advertising was the most convincing. After completion of the task, students review their work, sharing constructive feedback and agreeing on ways to improve collaborative work in future.

Improving own learning and performance

Students are required to:
1   set targets and plan how these will be met
2   take responsibility for their own learning and use plans to help meet targets and improve performance
3   review progress and establish evidence of achievements

All **Ánimo 1** units provide opportunities to meet these criteria through:

♦   **Clear objectives and means of reviewing progress**
Each unit begins with a list of objectives, providing clear information to students about what they will learn in the unit, including grammar and skills. In addition to these unit objectives, students should be encouraged to set their own personal targets relating to aspects of their performance that they want to improve, with an action plan showing how they intend to achieve the targets and how they will assess their progress. The *Repaso* sections at the end of each couple of units provide students with a means of reviewing their progress.

♦   **Strategies for improving performance**
All **Ánimo 1** units include *Técnica* sections, which suggest strategies and activities to help students develop as independent learners and improve aspects of their own performance. Strategies range from specific listening, speaking, reading and writing advice to tips on using dictionaries effectively and suggestions on recording and learning new language.

Problem solving

Although a modern foreign language course may not generate sufficient evidence to assess this key skill, language learning does provide opportunities to practise and develop problem-solving skills. For example, a 'problem' in language learning can take the form of any unknown word or phrase. If students are encouraged to 'work out' new language for themselves and take responsibility for their own learning instead of relying on teacher support, they develop problem-solving skills.

All **Ánimo 1** units provide opportunities for students to do this. In particular, the *Técnica* sections encourage students to become more independent in their language learning.

Information and communications technology

These notes provide a few examples of ways to use ICT with **Ánimo**. For more detailed information on current software and technologies, together with practical help and ideas on the use of ICT in the modern foreign languages classroom, you may find the following helpful:
- Becta (British Educational Communications and Technology Agency)
  www.becta.org.uk
- CILT (The National Centre for Languages)
  www.cilt.org.uk
- Languages ICT
  www.languages-ict.org.uk

Internet

Note on Internet safety: Before using the Internet with students, whether for online communication, the creation of web pages and blogs, or for research purposes, it is vital to be aware of safety issues. Guidance on this can be obtained from Becta (see website above).

Online communication

If your school has links with a partner school in a Spanish-speaking country, the Internet offers a range of ways in which your students can communicate with their Spanish counterparts, e.g. email, instant messaging, chat rooms, noticeboards and forums, audio- and video-conferencing, web pages and blogs. All these technologies enable the exchange of a wide range of information, from text and graphics to audio and video clips. They are extremely useful for motivating students, encouraging spontaneous communication and generating a source of additional teaching and learning material. The creation of web pages and blogs (e.g. to be viewed by a partner school in a Spanish-speaking country) provides students with a sense of purpose, since they are writing for a real audience.

There are many opportunities in **Ánimo 1** where online communication can be used to enhance the work of a unit, e.g.
- Unit 2, page 36, activity 1: As a follow-up to work on new technology, students could compare the survey findings with a Spanish partner class.
- Unit 8, page 111, activity 5b: As a follow-up to work on debating the differences between the generations, students could continue the debate with a Spanish partner class.
- Unit 9: Exchange information about school timetables and the Spanish and British education systems.

Internet research

The Internet can be a valuable research tool, giving both teachers and students easy access to authentic reading materials and cultural information about Spanish-speaking countries. Opportunities for students to research on the Internet occur throughout **Ánimo**. Themes include:
- Unit 3, page 47, activity 5: Spanish and Latin American film directors
- Unit 3, page 44, activity 1b: Students use the Internet to find out more information about a famous person of their choice.
- Unit 6, page 88, activity 1c: the Mediterranean diet
- Unit 9, page 124, activity 1: *telesecundaria*

Word-processing and text manipulation

Word-processing software allows text to be presented in a variety of forms that can be easily edited and manipulated. Words, phrases, sentences and paragraphs can be moved, changed, copied and highlighted, making it easier for students to experiment with language and to draft and redraft their work. Any written task can be completed on the computer, e.g.
- Unit 4, page 59, activity 4: Students write a letter defending the actions of young people.
- Unit 4, page 61, activity 4: Students write a report about a Spanish or Latin American celebrity.
- Unit 6, page 91, *Técnica* C: Students write a summary of the experiences of the three people on page 90, focusing on how their lives have changed.
- Unit 9. page 133, activity 3: Students write a text about the disadvantages and advantages of repeating a school year.

Desktop publishing

Desktop publishing software enables students to design sophisticated documents involving complex layout of text, clip art, digital photos and scanned images, e.g. brochures and leaflets, advertisements, posters, magazine-style articles and newsletters. Opportunities for students to use desktop publishing in **Ánimo** include:

♦ Unit 1, page 29, activity 4: Students design an advert to raise awareness of the importance of using a seatbelt when driving.
♦ Unit 4, page 67, activity 2b: Students design a leaflet to promote the moderate use of computer games.
♦ Unit 6, page 83, activity 3e: Students prepare an official public information notice warning about the risks of smoking whilst driving.

Databases and spreadsheets

Data-processing software allows text- and number-based information gathered by students, possibly during a class survey, to be entered into a database then sorted and analysed in different ways; spreadsheet software is more suitable for dealing with number-based (rather than text-based) data. Both of these technologies generate a range of opportunities for further language work, comparison and discussion of the data, etc.
Opportunities to use these technologies in **Ánimo** include:

♦ Unit 2, page 35, activity 5: After students have completed the questionnaire to see what type of internet user their fellow students are, the results could be fed into a database or recorded on a spreadsheet and used to generate further language work.
♦ Unit 4, page 57, activity 4: After doing the survey of the most popular activities for teenagers, students could compile a database of the results.

Presentation software

Presentation software (e.g. PowerPoint) allows students to create multimedia 'slides' combining text, images, sound and video clips, active links to web pages, animations, etc. The slides can be displayed to the whole class via a data projector and wall screen or interactive whiteboard. Themes for oral presentations in **Ánimo** include:

♦ Unit 1, page 25, activity 2b: censorship of advertising
♦ Unit 3, page 47, activity 5: Details about a famous Spanish or Latin American film director
♦ Unit 4, page 59, activity 3: Comparing the youth of today with the youth from the past

¿Ya lo sabías?

Nombre _____

1 Pablo is talking about what he does at the weekend. Fill each gap with a verb from the box, making sure you use the correct form of the present tense. *(10 marks)*

Normalmente los sábados por la mañana no (**1**) _____ mucho. A veces (**2**) _____ con mis amigos por la tarde y (**3**) _____ al tenis o al baloncesto. Por la noche siempre (**4**) _____ al cine o a la disco. Si (**5**) _____ una fiesta entonces (**6**) _____ ropa fina, si no (**7**) _____ llevar vaqueros o chándal. De todos modos los domingos (**8**) _____ día de (**9**) _____ con la familia y después de un buen almuerzo muchas veces (**10**) _____ hacer una siesta antes de pasear con mis padres.

hacer	tener	ir	ser	estar	preferir
jugar	querer	salir	ponerse		

2 Complete each sentence with the correct form of the adjective. *(10 marks)*

1 En mi casa tenemos (*mucho*) _____ animales.

2 Mi abuelo es una persona muy _____ (*generoso*).

3 Mis primos son todos bastante _____ (*joven*).

4 En otoño las hojas se ponen _____ (*marrón*) antes de caerse.

5 Juan es un _____ (*bueno*) amigo.

6 Mira _____ (*aquel*) nubes que se están acercando.

7 Lo siento, pero no hay _____ (*ninguno*) libro con ese título aquí.

8 En mi opinión los Beatles son _____ (*mejor*) que los Stones.

9 A mis amigos _____ (*galés*) les gusta el rugby.

10 Viven en el _____ (*tercero*) piso del nuevo edificio.

3 Complete the sentences with the correct pronouns. *(10 marks)*

1 Yo vivo en una casa pero _____ vivís en un apartamento.

2 ¿Qué es lo que _____ quieres de verdad?

3 Mire, señor, me parece que _____ está equivocado.

4 Normalmente me quedo en la cama los sábados y _____ levanto bastante tarde.

5 En cambio, los lunes como hay colegio, tenemos que levantar _____ temprano.

6 He perdido las gafas. No sé dónde _____ he puesto.

7 Acabo de comprar un coche. ¿Quieres ver _____?

8 Quiero mucho a mis abuelos y _____ escribo con frecuencia.

9 – ¿Cuándo vas a darle el regalo a Paco? – Acabo de dar _____.

10 – ¿Quién te da la paga? – Mis padres siempre _____ dan.

4 Use the clues to write sentences summarizing what you did last week at school. Follow the example and use the preterite tense. *(10 marks)*

Example: *coger, autobús, casa – Cogí el autobús delante de mi casa.*

1 llegar, al colegio

2 encontrarse con, el patio, recreo

3 tener, clase de deporte

4 no hacer, en clase

5 estar, durante, historia

6 comer, la cafetería

7 sacar, notas, química

8 ir, club de natación, polideportivo

9 ser, primero, grupo

10 jugar, partido de, con

¿Ya lo sabías?

Nombre _____

1 Translate the underlined parts of these sentences into Spanish. *(10 marks)*

1 <u>I was watching</u> television when my parents <u>arrived</u> home.

_____

2 <u>They were all asleep</u> when the burglars <u>entered</u> the house.

_____

3 What <u>were you listening</u> to when <u>I telephoned</u> you?

_____

4 <u>He was running</u> down the road when <u>he fell over</u>.

_____

5 <u>She was playing</u> tennis when <u>she hurt</u> her arm.

_____

6 <u>We all left</u> whilst <u>they were dancing</u>.

_____

7 Mother <u>shouted</u> for me to get up but <u>I was already getting dressed</u>.

_____

8 <u>It started to rain</u> just as <u>we were going out</u> to swim.

_____

9 <u>I set the table</u> whilst Peter <u>was preparing</u> the meal.

_____

10 <u>I wanted</u> to read while <u>you were all playing</u> cards.

_____

2 Complete these sentences with the correct form of the perfect tense. *(10 marks)*

1 ¿Qué _____ (*tú/hacer*) hoy por la tarde?

2 Mi amiga Juanita me _____ (*invitar*) a ir al cine con ella.

3 Más tarde _____ (*nosotros/salir*) a comer a un restaurante.

4 Como mis padres no estaban en casa les _____ (*escribir*) una nota.

5 No sé dónde _____ (*poner*) la bolsa.

6 Creo que la _____ (*perder*).

7 ¿Qué _____ (*tú/decir*) a tus padres?

8 Nada todavía, porque no les _____ (*yo/ver*).

9 No _____ (*ellos/volver*) a casa.

10 Hoy es fiesta y no _____ (*abrir*) el banco.

3 Enrique and Marta are discussing their future plans. Complete the sentences with the correct form of the future or conditional tense of the verb in brackets. *(10 marks)*

1 No tengo la menor idea de lo que _____ (*hacer*) el año que viene.

2 Yo tampoco pero _____ (*gustar*) viajar un poco.

3 Creo que _____ (*quedarse*) aquí para trabajar una temporada.

4 No sé si _____ (*tener*) suficiente dinero para estudiar.

5 Yo que tú _____ (*salir*) de este pueblo.

6 Bueno, bueno, te _____ (*decir*) lo que he decidido hacer más tarde.

7 ¿Tú crees que Pepe _____ (*querer*) acompañarme en mis viajes?

8 No se sabe nunca lo que _____ (*venir*) en el futuro.

9 Si saco buenas notas _____ (*poder*) seguir estudiando.

10 Mañana por la mañana _____ (*saber*) los resultados de los exámenes.

4 Use an appropriate form of the verb given in brackets to complete each sentence. *(10 marks)*

1 Ayer _____ (*llover*) tanto que no _____ (*poder*) salir.

2 Si _____ (*seguir*) haciendo mal tiempo _____ (*ir*) al cine esta tarde.

3 No _____ (*saber*) si _____ (*querer*) salir esta tarde.

4 Entonces _____ (*poder*) quedarnos en casa si _____ (*preferir*).

5 Vale, _____ (*ir*) a llamar a los chicos para ver si les _____ (*gustar*) jugar a las cartas.

6 El otro día cuando _____ (*estar*) en clase Miguel me _____ (*invitar*) a salir con él.

7 ¿Y qué _____ (*hacer*)? ¿_____ (*salir*) con Miguel o _____ (*quedarse*) con Felipe?

8 Pues no sé, porque _____ (*pensar*) que _____ (*ser*) mejor buscar un novio diferente.

9 ¿Qué me _____ (*decir*)? En mi opinión _____ (*deber*) ser honesta con Felipe.

10 De acuerdo, siempre _____ (*ser*) buenos amigos pero ahora _____ (*sentirse*) aburrida.

Lesson Plan

Date :	Teacher :	Class :

Objectives	Resources

Objectives for Students	Notes/Reminders

Starter:

Teaching sequence:

Differentiation/Extension:

Plenary:

Homework:

¿Ya lo sabías? – diagnostic tests

Depending on your groups for AS, Hojas 1 and 2 could be given to students after a brief revision session of the major grammatical points for GCSE. Section 1 on Hoja 1 should take 20 minutes and section 2 on Hoja 2 about 30 minutes. The results should indicate where the major weaknesses are and grammar revision and teaching could begin from these areas. In addition to these tests, you may wish to provide students with a written task to assess the fluency and accuracy of their written work.

Hoja 1 ¿Ya lo sabías?

Answers:

1 *1 hago 2 salgo 3 juego 4 voy 5 tengo
6 me pongo 7 prefiero 8 es 9 estar 10 quiero*

There are 10 marks for this activity. If students score less than 6 marks, refer them to page 162, section 9.2 in the **Ánimo 1** Students' Book.

Answers:

2 *1 muchos 2 generoso 3 jóvenes 4 marrones
5 buen 6 aquellas 7 ningún 8 mejore
9 galeses 10 tercer*

There are 10 marks for this activity. If students score less than 6 marks, refer them to page 156, section 2 in the **Ánimo 1** Students' Book.

Answers:

3 *1 vosotros 2 tú 3 usted 4 me 5 nos
6 las 7 lo 8 les 9 selo 10 me la*

There are 12 marks (2 each for 9 and 10) for this activity. If students score less than 8 marks, refer them to page 159, section 6 in the **Ánimo 1** Students' Book.

Suggested answers:

4 *1 Llegué tarde/a tiempo al colegio esta mañana.
2 Me encontré con mis amigos en el patio durante el recreo.
3 Tuve una clase de deporte por la tarde.
4 No hice nada en la clase de dibujo.
5 Estuve aburrida durante historia.
6 Comí en la cafetería al mediodía.
7 Saqué buenas notas por la tarea de química.
8 Fui al club de natación en el nuevo polideportivo.
9 Fui la primera del grupo a terminar.
10 Jugué un buen partido de baloncesto con el equipo.*

There are 10 marks for each correct preterite in this activity. If students score less than 6 marks, refer them to page 162, section 9.4 in the **Ánimo 1** Students' Book.

Hoja 2 ¿Ya lo sabías?

Answers:

1 *1 veía/estaba viendo – llegaron
2 dormían/estaban durmiendo – entraron
3 escuchabas/estabas escuchando – llamé por teléfono
4 corría/estaba corriendo – se cayó
5 jugaba/estaba jugando – se hizo mal
6 nos fuimos – bailaban/estaban bailando
7 gritó – ya me vestía/estaba vistiéndome
8 comenzó/se puso a llover – salíamos/íbamos
9 puse la mesa – preparaba/estaba preparando
10 quería – jugabáis/estabáis jugando*

There are 20 marks (1 for each correct verb/tense) for this activity. If students score less than 12 marks, refer them to pages 163 and 164 in the **Ánimo 1** Students' Book.

Answers:

2 *1 has hecho 2 ha invitado 3 hemos salido
4 he escrito 5 he puesto 6 he perdido
7 has dicho 8 he visto 9 han vuelto
10 se ha abierto*

There are 10 marks for this activity. If students score less than 6 marks, refer them to page 164, section 9.10 in the **Ánimo 1** Students' Book.

Answers:

3 *1 haré 2 me gustaría 3 me quedaré 4 tendré
5 saldría 6 diré 7 querrá 8 vendrá
9 podría/podré 10 sabremos.*

There are 10 marks for this activity. If students score less than 6 marks, refer them to page 164, section 9.7 and 9.9 in the Ánimo Students' Book.

Answers:

4 *1 llovía/llovió – pude 2 sigue – iré 3 sé– querré
4 podemos – prefieres 5 voy – gustaría
6 estuve/estaba – invitó 7 harás – saldrás – te quedarás 8 pienso – es será 9 dices – debes
10 hemos sido – me siento.*

There are 20 marks for this activity. If students score less than 12 marks, refer them to the previously mentioned sections and pages in the **Ánimo 1** Students' Book.

**Having completed the diagnostic tests, all students should familiarize themselves with the layout and features of the Students' Book. Encourage students to discuss the themes covered and to pick out those they are already familiar with and to say which topics interest them most and why.
They should also look at the grammar summary in the table of contents on pages 2 and 3 and indicate which aspects they feel confident about, which they feel they need to revise and which are new to them.**

Puente

Unit objectives

By the end of this unit students will be able to:
- Describe the area they live in
- Speak and write about a Spanish-speaking region or country
- Speak and write about themselves
- Research key people and places in the Spanish-speaking world
- Write a profile of the above

Grammar

By the end of this unit students will be able to:
- Recognise and use the present, perfect and preterite tenses
- Recognise the difference between *ser* and *estar* and use them correctly
- Make comparisons
- Recognise and use gender markers correctly
- Make adjectives agree, shorten, and place them correctly

Skills

By the end of this unit students will be able to:
- Write a brief description
- Record and learn vocabulary effectively
- Pronounce the five vowel sounds

Resources

- Students' Book pages 6 and 7
- CD 1, track 2

1a Students look at the photos and see how many they recognise. This could be done as a whole class task or as individuals to elicit just how much background knowledge students already possess.

 1b Students listen and match the photos to the commentary to gain a general impression, and identify the photo being talked about.

Answers: 1 *C*　2 *A*　3 *F*　4 *E*　5 *B*　6 *D*

 1c Students listen again for detail and phrases with the appropriate photo.

Answers: 1 *C*　2 *D*　3 *A*　4 *B*　5 *E*　6 *A*
　　　　　7 *C*　8 *F*　9 *D*　10 *E*　11 *F*　12 *B*

P6, actividad 1b

1 España tiene un paisaje muy variado. Los Picos de Europa – las montañas más antiguas de Europa – se levantan a unos 1.000 metros en los valles verdes del norte del país. El sureste, sin embargo, es casi un desierto.

---

2 Este edificio tan raro es un símbolo de la creatividad y el carácter independiente de los catalanes. Si subes las más de 400 escaleras hasta lo alto de una de las ocho torres ya acabadas, tendrás una vista sin igual de la animada ciudad de Barcelona.

3 El tango es uno de los bailes más famosos y sensuales del mundo. Tiene su origen en el barrio del puerto de Buenos Aires, la capital de Argentina. En todo momento se pueden ver parejas bailando en la calle acompañadas de la música del bandoneón.

4 Uno de los pintores más famosos del mundo, Pablo Ruiz Picasso, pintó este cuadro en 1937 después del bombardeo atroz del pueblo vasco de Guernica durante la Guerra Civil española.

5 Construido principalmente durante el siglo XV, este misterioso lugar fue usado como palacio del emperador Inca y como santuario religioso. Se considera una obra maestra de la arquitectura y la ingeniería. Estas ruinas están en la lista del Patrimonio de la Humanidad desde 1983 y se han convertido en uno de los destinos turísticos más populares del mundo. Son un icono nacional del Perú.

6 Desde 1977, dos años después de la muerte del dictador Franco, España es una democracia parlamentaria y monárquica. El rey, Juan Carlos I, vive con su esposa, la reina Sofía, en el palacio de la Zarzuela, un edificio modesto comparado con el Palacio Real de Madrid y otros palacios de Europa. Sus tres hijos Elena, Cristina y Felipe están casados, ¡y les han dado muchos nietos!

1d Students match the titles to the four photos. Note there are two extra photos.

Answers:
Una iglesia extraordinaria – A
Antiguo monumento de los Incas – B
Cuadro emblemático de Picasso – E
Un baile sensual – F

1e Students make up titles for the remaining two photos.

Possible answers could be:
La familia real;　Los Picos de Europa

1f Students follow the example and write a sentence or sentences about the photos.

Técnica

Discuss the various research methods, and if necessary, pair up students so that the more confident help the weaker ones on this aspect.

Students present their research to the rest of the class in as much, or as little, detail as appropriate. They decide on their final top ten images to represent the Spanish-speaking world.

Recorriendo las Españas

Grammar focus
- The formation and use of the present tense
- The different uses of *ser* and *estar*

Skills focus
- Research skills

Key language
- *soler* + infinitive
- *ser* and *estar*
- points of compass: *norte, sur, este, oeste*

Resources
- Students' Book pages 8 and 9
- CD 1, tracks 3–4
- Grammar Workbook page 32

 1a Having studied the map for a few minutes, students listen and identify who is speaking and where they are from – their region.

P 8, actividad 1a

1 Saludos desde el Principado de Asturias – me llamo Victoria.
2 ¡Hola! Me llamo Omar y vivo en Murcia, en el sureste del país.
3 Y yo me llamo Maribel y vivo en Estepona, en Andalucía, en el sur.
4 Bienvenidos a Menorca, una de las islas Baleares – soy Jordi.
5 Y yo soy Raúl, y saludo a todos desde Zaragoza, la capital de Aragón.
6 Y por último voy yo – Silvana. Os saludo desde Lanzarote, en las Islas Canarias.

Answers:
1 *Victoria, Asturias*
2 *Omar, Murcia*
3 *Maribel, Andalucía*
4 *Jordi, Menorca (Baleares)*
5 *Raúl, Aragón*
6 *Silvana, Lanzarote (Canarias)*

 1b Students listen and take notes about each speaker. This prepares for Activity 1c. So it may help to go through the questions of 1c beforehand to help students to focus on the relevant information.

P 8, actividad 1b

1
- Bueno, Silvana, ¿cómo es la vida en las Islas Canarias?
- Pues, Lanzarote, donde vivo yo, es la cuarta isla más grande de las siete islas Canarias y la más bonita. Arrecife, su capital en la costa este, es bastante comercial y moderna.
- ¿Qué hay de interés en la isla?
- A los turistas les gusta mucho visitar el Parque Nacional de Timanfaya porque les parece muy extraño con su paisaje volcánico.
- ¿A ti, qué te gusta hacer?
- A mí me gusta el arte y suelo visitar a menudo el museo de César Manrique, nuestro pintor más famoso.

2
- Maribel, hay mucho turismo donde vives tú, ¿verdad?
- Sí, porque hace calor y sol casi todo el año, sobre todo en Sevilla, la capital de Andalucía.
- ¿Qué sueles hacer en tu pueblo?
- No hay mucho que hacer para los jóvenes como yo si no te gusta la playa o el deporte y a mí no me gusta ni lo uno ni lo otro.
- Pero ¿qué hay de interés para los turistas entonces?
- Hay varios restaurantes buenos y se pueden visitar los pueblos blancos en las montañas que hay cerca de Ronda.

3
- Raúl, ¿qué nos puedes decir de Zaragoza?
- Es la capital de Aragón en el norte de España. Está situada sobre el río Ebro, en un valle casi en el centro de la región y alrededor todo parece un desierto.
- ¿Te gusta vivir allí?
- Sí, porque es una importante ciudad militar tanto para el Ejército como para las fuerzas aéreas. Está a igual distancia de Madrid, Barcelona, Valencia y Bilbao y ahora el tren de alta velocidad, el AVE, pasa por aquí.
- ¿Hay algo interesante para los turistas allí?
- Sí ... la famosa Basílica Católica de Nuestra Señora del Pilar y las ruinas romanas pero para mí lo más importante es el estadio de fútbol del Real Zaragoza.

4
- ¿Dónde vives exactamente, Victoria, y qué se hace en Asturias?
- Vivo cerca de la capital, Oviedo, en una ciudad que se llama Gijón, que está a orillas del mar y donde hay un puerto industrial. Asturias tiene valles verdes entre montañas grises. Hago bastante deporte y me encanta el surf. Los fines de semana, mis amigos y yo solemos pasarlos en la playa. Lo bueno es que hay mucho de interés para el turista pero lo malo es que estamos un poco aislados.

5
- Omar, ¿cómo es tu pueblo? ¿Y qué te gusta hacer allí?
- Lorca es un pueblo que fue fundado en tiempos de los moros donde hay muchos cultivos de frutas y legumbres. Cuando era joven solía jugar al baloncesto pero hoy prefiero la música y suelo practicar con un grupo llamado Los Tarifeños. Murcia, la capital de la región, tiene muchos monumentos antiguos.

6
- Jordi, háblame de tu región.
- Vivo en Sant Lluís, una bonita aldea no muy lejos de Maó, la capital de Menorca. Tiene unos 3.000 habitantes nada más y normalmente es muy tranquila, pintoresca y encantadora. No me gusta el verano cuando llegan los turistas haciendo ruido y dejando basura por todas partes. Aquí se suele comer muchos mariscos y se vive muy bien.

1c In pairs, students take turns to be interviewee and interviewer. They use the questions provided.

2a Students study their notes and listen again to the previous transcript in order to elicit phrases and vocabulary that best suit their own situation.

2b Students then use the questions from 1c to create a dialogue, with a partner, about themselves. They should consult the *frases clave* to help them as well.

3 Students write a brief description of their own region using all the relevant vocabulary and phrases gained so far.

Create text files so that students practise writing using text manipulation. The transcripts could be used as a basis for this activity.

4 This task extends and develops students' ability to research and elicit relevant information.

Gramática

The present tense – its formation and uses. Refer students to the relevant grammar section of the Students' Book.
Radical or stem changing verbs – ensure students understand how they are formed and how they are presented in a dictionary.

A *vuelvo vuelves vuelve volvemos volvéis vuelven*
B *cojo coges coge etc.*
   sigo, sigues, sigue etc.
C *digo, voy, estoy, soy, pongo, vengo*

Ser and *estar* – Ask students to provide examples of the different uses to ensure they are fully competent and not just making guesses about which one to use.

D Using the map, students can quiz each other:

A: *¿Dónde está Zaragoza?* – **B:** *Está en el norte de España.*
A: *¿Cómo es?* – **B:** *Es una ciudad grande.*

If students are not familiar with the map of Spain, this will help to orientate them as well.

E Students write their own sentences to illustrate the differences using the vocabulary provided.

Otros países hispanohablantes

Grammar focus
- Comparatives
- Cardinal and ordinal numbers

Skills focus
- More research

Key language
- *más ... que / menos que; tan como / tanto como*
- *mejor, peor, mayor, menor*
- numbers and agreements

Resources
- Students' Book pages 10 and 11
- CD 1, tracks 5–7
- Grammar Workbook page 12

1a Students study the map of Latin America to familiarise themselves with it and gauge just how much prior knowledge they already have. They then listen and note the names of the countries mentioned and locate them on the map.

P 10, actividad 1a

- La parte de América donde se habla español es un subcontinente enorme que empieza en el cono sur, compuesto por Chile, Argentina, Paraguay y Uruguay. Sigue con Bolivia, Perú y Ecuador con sus islas Galápagos en la parte central y Colombia y Venezuela en el norte. Luego se continúa por el istmo de Panamá a través de Costa Rica, Nicaragua, Honduras, El Salvador y Guatemala hasta llegar a México.
- No hay que olvidar las islas caribeñas de Cuba, Puerto Rico y la República Dominicana y, por supuesto, gran parte de los Estados Unidos donde hay una importante representación latina.

Answers:

Chile, Argentina, Paraguay, Uruguay, Bolivia, Perú, Ecuador, Colombia, Venezuela, Panamá, Costa Rica, Nicaragua, Honduras, El Salvador,

Guatemala, México, Cuba, Puerto Rica, República Dominicana, Estados Unidos.

1b In pairs, students play the game of "True or False" again to familiarise themselves with basic information about Latin American countries and their capitals. They should try to do this from memory after a few turns each. This also helps to reaffirm the verbs *ser* and *estar* plus the points on the compass from the previous spread.

Gramática

Comparatives. Refer students to the relevant grammar section of the Students' Book.

2 They complete the text with the missing numbers. Depending on how competent students are with numbers, revise the ordinal and cardinal numbers in the Grammar Box before or after they have completed this task.

P 10, actividad 2

– Dicen que mi país es uno de los más bonitos y pacíficos de Latinoamérica y francamente estoy de acuerdo. Se sitúa entre dos océanos, El Pacífico y el Atlántico o el mar Caribe y tiene 3.800.000 habitantes que viven en **51 km²** de tierra – pero no es un país tan pequeño como El Salvador.

– Vivo en Puntarenas, un pueblo costeño del Pacífico a unos **110 km** de la capital, San José. La mayoría de los habitantes (los ticos) son descendientes de los españoles pero un **2%** son indígenas y hablan el idioma nahua (que es parecido a la lengua azteca) y en la costa hay un grupo de ascendencia africana que habla inglés-patois.

– Costa Rica es un tesoro ecológico – un **5%** de la biodiversidad del mundo entero se encuentra aquí y un **25%** de la tierra está protegida y forma parte de alguno de los parques nacionales del país. Hay una enorme variedad de ecosistemas – bosques nubosos, selva tropical, playas extensas, manglares y volcanes. El punto más alto se llama Monte Chiripó y está a **3819 m**. De la historia del país lo más importante es que desde **1948** no hemos tenido ejército – por eso nos llaman la pequeña Suiza – ¡y uno de nuestros presidentes era un poeta famoso!

Answers:
The answers are in bold in the transcript.

Gramática

Cardinal numbers. Students should be familiar with numbers by now but will need a reminder about agreements especially of number 1.

Ordinal numbers. Remind students about adjectives which shorten before a masculine noun. There is an opportunity here to remind students about percentages, fractions and other number usages.

3a This is a more challenging listening task but if students focus on the headings provided they should be able to make notes under them in English or Spanish. There is an opportunity here to use the transcript for a text manipulation activity as well.

P 11, actividad 3a

– Colombia está en el norte de Sudamérica. Una de sus costas limita con el Mar Caribe y la otra con el Océano Pacífico. Es un país grande con una superficie de 1.138.400 km², similar a Francia, España y la parte oeste de Alemania juntos. Solamente Brasil, Argentina y Perú son más grandes que Colombia.

– Allí viven unos 40 millones de habitantes. Muchos se llaman 'mestizos' porque son de raza mixta – blancos, negros, indios.

– Bogotá, la capital, está a unos 2.600 metros de altura en los Andes – las montañas que atraviesan el país de norte a sur. Durante gran parte del año cae una lluvia fina sobre la ciudad.

– Es un país que goza de todos los climas y por eso produce toda clase de frutas, flores y legumbres. Tiene fama por su algodón fino, su rico café y sus esmeraldas incomparables. La industria petrolera y mineral es bastante importante y hay minas de carbón enormes en el norte.

– Su cultura representa las diversas gentes que la componen, por ejemplo, con sus bailes y ritmos africanos de la costa y su música andina. En el Museo de Oro se pueden ver cantidades de artefactos precolombinos.

– Es una república democrática y sólo ha pasado por cuatro años de dictadura en su historia, un tiempo muy corto comparado con otros países sudamericanos.

– Sin embargo, el mundo entero la conoce más por la violencia y por las drogas que por los muchos millones de colombianos honrados y trabajadores que viven allí entre un paisaje fantástico y variado.

3b Using the research skills already established, students research a Latin American country of their choice. Using the examples of Costa Rica and Colombia already presented, they make an oral presentation to the class.

4a Students read this letter and complete the personal details for Roberto.

Answers:
Nombre: Roberto. Edad: 17 años. Nacionalidad: peruano. Familia: 2 hermanos, 3 hermanas.

Aficiones: senderismo, vela, pesca, buceo.
Profesión: estudiante; Idiomas: Español y Quechua.

4b Students note details from the letter and write a brief description of Roberto.

4c Before completing this task, students could make up personal descriptions of classmates and guess who is being described to help them revise useful vocabulary and phrases. Students compose a letter following the model provided containing their own personal details.

Caras conocidas

Grammar focus
♦ Perfect tense
♦ Preterite tense

Key language
reconocer, elegir, escoger, el baile, bailar,
el bailarín, ambos/as, haber (se)

Resources
♦ Students' Book pages 12 and 13
♦ CD 1, tracks 8–9
♦ Grammar Workbook pages 38–39

1a Students look at the photos and see how many faces they know. The personalities are: Antonio Banderas, Penélope and Mónica Cruz, Salma Hayek, Rafael Nadal, Jennifer Lopez, Carlos Acosta, Che Guevara.

This is only a sample of Spanish-speaking personalities which may or may not be familiar to UK students. Point out that Spanish or Latin American students could well create a very different sample.

 1b Students listen and identify the person being discussed.

P 12, actividad 1b

– A ver, ¿a quién habéis elegido para representar al mundo hispano? Clara, tú primero.
– Pues, he escogido a Carlos Acosta, el bailarín cubano, sin dudar, porque me parece que ha hecho mucho por el baile tanto contemporáneo como clásico.
– Explícanos un poco más.
– Bueno, aunque nació de una familia pobre de La Habana, la capital de Cuba, y era uno de once hermanos, se ha dedicado al baile que allí se considera un verdadero arte tanto para hombres como para mujeres.

– ¿Entonces es parecido a nuestro Joaquín Cortés?
– Pues sí, en parte, pero me gusta más su estilo; es más elegante y atlético y aunque soy española no me gusta mucho el flamenco. Prefiero el baile clásico.
– Muy bien. Y tú, Belén: ¿Has pensado en alguien?
– Sí, señora, pero no he podido escoger entre las dos hermanas Cruz porque las dos me gustan igualmente.
– ¿Y eso por qué?
– Ay, porque son tan elegantes y guapas además de ser buenas actrices. Penélope siempre ha recibido más atención porque es la mayor pero Mónica, su hermana menor, también está empezando a ganar fama.
– Vale, vale y Fabián: me imagino que habrás escogido a un deportista, ¿no?
– Claro, claro – es todo lo que me importa – pero yo tampoco podía escoger entre el fútbol y el tenis.
– ¿Y qué has escogido por fin?
– A Rafa Nadal aunque Cesc Fábregas también me parece increíble deportista. Ambos son disciplinados y están totalmente dedicados a su carrera; ambos son jóvenes y ambiciosos sin ser orgullosos; ambos han triunfado en su deporte. ¿Qué más quiere?
– No se puede pedir más, la verdad. Bueno, ¿y tú, Manuel?
– Bueno, pues, como me fascina el arte y también el cine he decidido escoger a Salma Hayek por su papel como Frida Kahlo. Las dos son mujeres de carácter fuerte.
– Interesante. Y por fin, Milagros: preséntanos tu personaje.
– Yo sé que murió hace años pero para mí el Ché Guevara aún vive. Su foto ha llegado a ser un icono para mucha gente. Es un espíritu libre.
– Está bien; habéis hecho muy buen trabajo. Ahora vamos a buscar personajes históricos que influyeron la vida hispana ...

1c Students answer the questions.

Answers:

Clara – Carlos Acosta; *ha bailado; le gusta su estilo*
Belén – Penélope y Mónica Cruz; *son actrices; son las dos elegantes y guapas*
Fabián – Rafael Nadal; *ha jugado al tenis; es disciplinado y dedicado*

1d Students complete the personal details for Antonio Banderas and Jennifer López.

1e Students play a game of "True and False" describing the faces. They could also bring in more photos of faces to extend this activity. And/or use relevant historical characters if time allows.

Gramática

Compound tenses using *haber* – the perfect tense.
Refer students to the relevant grammar section of the Students' Book.

Answers:

1 *Aunque ha bailado por todo el mundo siempre ha regresado a la Habana cada año.*
2 *¿A quién has escogido?*
3 *¿Por qué te ha gustado?*
4 *Como siendo hermana mayor ha recibido más atención que su hermana menor.*
5 *Su foto ha llegado a ser un icono para mucha gente.*

2a Students listen a first time to gain the gist and focus on the interrogative words used.

P 13, actividad 2a

– A los veintidós años se hizo con la victoria más dulce de su vida ante las narices de su gran ídolo – les presento a Fernando Alonso, el ganador más joven de la historia de la Fórmula 1. ¿Qué signo es usted?
– Pues, nací el 29 de julio de 1981, así que soy Leo.
– ¿De qué parte de España es usted?
– Soy de Oviedo, capital del Principado de Asturias, en el norte de España.
– ¿Cuál fue su primer premio?
– Bueno, obtuve mi primera victoria en karting.
– ¿Cuántos años tenía?
– Tenía unos trece años, creo.
– ¿Por qué cambió del karting a la Fórmula 1?
– Porque es un progreso natural si uno es fanático del deporte de automovilismo.
– ¿Cuándo hizo su primera carrera en Fórmula 1?
– Fue en Melbourne, Australia, en 2001.
– ¿Quién es su ídolo?
– Aparte de mi padre, es sin duda Michael Schuhmacher – y también tengo respeto al colombiano Juan Pablo Montoya.
– ¿Cómo se sintió al ganar en Hungría en 2003?
– Muy orgulloso de ser el primer español en subir al podio.
– Así es y enhorabuena – felicitaciones a otro pionero del deporte español.

2b Students listen a second time and note down the full question form.

2c Students then choose the correct answer.

Answers:

D;   B;   H;   E;
F;   A;   C;   G

2d Students practise the full dialogue.

3a Students read the brief text about Mario Testino, another Peruvian, and complete his personal details, following the headings of Roberto on page 11 task 4a.

Answers:

Nombre – Mario Testino; Edad – students work this out from 1954; Nacionalidad – peruano; Familia – dos hermanas; ficiones –gastronomía; Profesión – fotógrafo; Idiomas – español, inglés, francés

3b Students research details about other famous personalities and make an oral presentation to the class. They then go on to decide on a final top ten list.

3c Students write a profile of their favourite Spanish-speaking personality and prepare to be interviewed by their partner.

Gramática

The preterite tense – the regular form.
Refer students to the relevant grammar section of the Students' Book.
Students will already be quite familiar with the first and third person singular but now they need to be sure they can manage the full paradigm.

A

sacar; pagar; empezar; averiguar; leer; oír; caer; creer

Ask students to provide further examples of their own.

B

nació; estudió; viajó; se instaló; se hizo; publicó

C

nací; cambió; sintió

Depending on how confident students feel about past tenses, work can be done on contrasting the perfect and preterite tenses at this stage, or left until the grammar in action page.

La España actual

Grammar focus
♦ Adjectives

Key language
las panales solares, los toldos, las vegas, veloz, un central

Resources
♦ Students' Book pages 14 and 15
♦ CD 1, track 10
♦ Grammar Workbook page 10

1a Students study the photos and discuss their significance and say if they recognise any of them. They then listen and indicate which image is being described.

P 14, actividad 1a

1 En más de 44 países del mundo Zara ha revolucionado el concepto de la moda rápida a buen precio.

2 En dos horas 25 minutos el tren de Alta Velocidad Española, el AVE, hace el viaje de Madrid a Sevilla.

3 Compara el tradicional cultivo antiguo del olivo con la nueva tecnología agrícola bajo toldos plásticos que hoy en día 'decoran' las vegas.

4 La Ciudad de las artes y las ciencias fue un concepto futurístico del arquitecto valenciano Santiago Calatrava.

5 Cerca de Sevilla hay una torre muy alta que se levanta entre 624 paneles solares.

6 Nombrado mejor cocinero del mundo por dos años seguidos, Ferrán Adriá celebra la cocina española.

7 Ya sea en un parque temático o con bailes y trajes típicos, los españoles saben celebrar sus fiestas.

1b Students choose a suitable title for each photo.

A 4; B 5; C 6; D 1; E 2; F 7; G 3

1c Students read the short texts and match them up to the relevant photo.

Answers: 1 *F*   2 *D*   3 *A*   4 *C*

1d Students practise their research skills again to find out more information about the remaining three photos – Valencia, fiestas/entertainment and Zara.

Gramática

Adjectives. Refer students to the relevant grammar section in the Students' Book.
Students will be quite familiar by now with the rules for agreement of adjectives, but they will need more practice on the position of adjectives.

A Students find examples in the texts and also make up further examples of their own.

Gramática en acción

Resources

♦ Students' Book page 16

A

Students write down examples for each of the typical endings working from memory. They compare their

list with that of a partner. Check each list or ask students to share them with the rest of the class. The student who ends up with the longest list, that no other student has, is declared the winner.

B

Students compile a list from the texts and then look for exceptions to the rule and learn them.

C

Refer to page 147 of the grammar section and ensure that students understand why this happens and can give further examples.

D

1 *preterite*
2 *perfect*
3 *perfect*
4 *preterite*
5 *preterite, perfect*
6 *perfect*
7 *preterite*
8 *preterite, perfect*

E

1 *ganó*
2 *ha ganado*
3 *ha bailado*
4 *bailó*
5 *me levanté, no me he lavado*
6 *he hecho*
7 *hice*
8 *comí, no he comido*

A escoger

Resources

♦ Students' Book page 17
♦ CD 1, tracks 11–13

1a Focusing on the three questions, students listen for detail.

P 17, actividad 1a

A La estatua de Cristóbal Colón se levanta a unos 52 metros al final de las Ramblas mirando hacia el mar; junto a él, la Pinta, el famoso barco que le llevó a descubrir América.

B Esta foto demuestra una estatua del célebre político y revolucionario mexicano Emiliano Zapata. Nacido cerca de Ayala (Morelos) en México en 1883, fue promotor de la reforma agraria. Proclamó el plan de Ayala en 1911 que exigía tierras para los campesinos. Murió asesinado en 1919.

Answers:

1 *Cristóbal Colón*   2 *Barcelona* 3 *descubrió América*

2 *Emiliano Zapata*   2 *México*   3 *revolucionario*

1b Students write a few more details about each photo.

Answers:

A *estatua; 52 metros de altura; final de las Ramblas; su barco La Pinta*

B *1883–1919; reforma agraria; murió asesinado*

2 Students listen and make notes on each of the three regions: Andalucía; Galicia, Castilla La Mancha.

> P 17, actividad 2
>
> – Andalucía es la comunidad autónoma más grande de España y cuenta con unos 7.600.000 habitantes. Las ocho provincias que componen la región van desde Cádiz, en la costa atlántica, hasta Almería, en la costa mediterránea. En Andalucía residen todos los estereotipos de España – flamenco, guitarra, pueblos blancos, fiestas religiosas y gitanos, turistas y tapas. Allí encontrarás una fusión de culturas – la cultura mora con la judía y la cristiana. Los cultivos de olivos marcan el paisaje.
> – Galicia, tal vez la región menos descubierta por los turistas y aislada en la punta noroeste, es la parte más verde del país. Allí se encuentra la tumba de Santiago de Compostela. La gente celta se ganan la vida en las rías de la costa atlántica, abundantes en mariscos y pescado. Pontevedra es el puerto pesquero más importante de España.
> – Castilla la Mancha, meseta abierta salpicada de molinos de viento y castillos, ofrece una imagen clásica de España. Aquí encontrarás los viñedos más extensos del mundo y en el otoño los campos se vuelven violetas con el color del azafrán. En esta parte central del país hay también dos parques nacionales, las Tablas de Damiel y Cabañeros.

3 Students revise the unit. This activity could be done as a team game or in pairs.

4 Students write a full self portrait. They could follow a writing frame or model.

Se pronuncia así

Students use the recording to practise vowel sounds. Encourage them to practise in front of a mirror so that they not only feel the shape of the mouth but see it as well. They can prepare a recording of their own with pauses for repetition.

> P 17, Se pronuncia así
>
> Alba Arbalaez abre su abanico amarillo amablemente.
> Enrique Esquivel escoge el edredón más elegante.
> Inés Iglesias indica que es imposible ingresar allí.
> Óscar Ordóñez odia las hojas otoñales.
> Umberto Umbral usa un uniforme ultramoderno.

Técnica

Go through the grammar learning tips to make students aware of just how much they can do for themselves to organise their learning and encourage them to help each other by testing and swapping learning cards.

Encourage students to follow the advice on vocabulary learning and recording. They should devise their own ways of doing this as well.

Unidad 1 Los medios de comunicación

Unit objectives

By the end of this unit students will be able to:

♦ Talk and write about TV ratings, channels and programmes
♦ Discuss the role of radio and TV
♦ Discuss the impact of advertising on people's lives
♦ Discuss the role of the written press

Grammar

By the end of this unit students will be able to:

♦ Use different negatives
♦ Use verbs of like / dislike + infinitive or noun
♦ Recognise and use the irregular preterite (radical changes)
♦ Understand how to form, and when to use, the present subjunctive with verbs of wanting, requesting and advising
♦ Extend vocabulary using suffixes, antonyms and synonyms

Skills

By the end of this unit students will be able to:

♦ Take notes when listening
♦ Recognise different registers of language

Resources

♦ Students' Book pages 18 and 19
♦ CD 1, track 14

This spread introduces the topic.

1 Students complete the quiz.

2 Students discuss which of the media types best inform people. They then discuss different types of advertising.

3 Prepare students for doing some on-line research for this exercise. Students make sure they know the vocabulary for the different types of TV programmes. They then research on *laguiatv.com* for titles of programmes for each category and give an equivalent sort of programme in English.

Gramática

Negative. Students study the grammar box on negatives. For some students this will be a revision process, and for others a new learning one.

 A When they are sufficiently familiar with the negatives, they listen to the recording and identify the negative words used.

Answers:

1 *nunca, no*
2 *nadie, ni siquiera, jamás*
3 *no–nada, ni–ni, no–ningún, ninguna, nada*
4 *tampoco*

B Students note down the form of negative used.

Answers:

1 *c and a* **2** *c, d, c* **3** *b, d, b, d* **4** *a, d*

P 19, actividad A

1
– ¿Qué estás viendo?
– Deportes.
– Nunca veo programas de deportes, no me gustan.
– Pues, a mí me encantan.

2
– A nadie le gusta el canal 5, ni siquiera a mi abuelo.
– Estoy de acuerdo, jamás lo veo.

3
– No hay nada en la tele esta noche.
– Tienes razón, ni deporte ni música …
– No hay ningún concurso, ninguna telenovela – en fin, nada.

4
– A mí no me gustan las noticias. ¿A ti te gustan?
– A mí tampoco.

 C Finally students invent similar dialogues and discuss their own viewing preferences.

Los programas más vistos

Grammar focus

♦ Verbs of like / dislike + infinitive or noun
♦ Verbs + infinitive

Skills focus

♦ Listening and taking notes

Key language

♦ *gustar* and similar verbs + noun or infinitive

♦ *poder* and similar verbs + infinitive

Resources

♦ Students' Book pages 20 and 21
♦ CD 1, tracks 15–16
♦ Hojas 1, 5
♦ Grammar workbook page 64

1 Students read the letters page of a TV magazine and answer the questions. This provides them with key vocabulary and phrases they will need for activity 2.

Answers should include:

1 *porque tratan a la gente como cifras y dinero; no ponen atención a la calidad ni creatividad de los programas*
2 Student's own opinion and wording
3 Student's own opinion and wording
4 Student's own opinion and wording
5 Encourage students to write their own minisode of a familiar soap.
6 Students give their own opinion about reality TV shows.
7 Students give their own opinion about 15 minutes of fame.

Gramática

Verbs such as *gustar* which take either a noun or an infinitive.
Students will think they know all about this already but no doubt they will need reminding about agreement of plural or singular.

A Students make up sentences of their own to illustrate that they know how to use this construction.

Verbs which take an infinitive.
(Refer students to the relevant grammar sections of the Student's Book and the Grammar Workbook.)

B Students write sentences about the role of television using the verbs listed.

 2a Students listen and decide whether the speakers prefer radio or television and note their reasons.

P 21, actividad 2a

1 A mí me encanta la tele porque las imágenes me distraen y hoy en día hay una gran variedad de canales con programas serios o frívolos y hay algo para todo el mundo.
2 Pues no sé, pero me parece a mí que te concentras más con la radio, sobre todo si estás escuchando las noticias o música.
3 Vale, vale, de acuerdo que ambas informan, entretienen y relajan pero con la radio tienes que usar la imaginación mientras que la tele te lo da todo hecho.

---

4 Creo que a veces esto no es bueno, sobre todo cuando se trata de niños. Ellos ven muchas cosas que no deberían y eso les afecta. También creo que pasan demasiadas horas embobados delante de la pantalla.
5 Me parece muy acertado y es que todos perdemos muchas horas al día delante de la caja tonta. En cambio, con la radio no desperdicias el tiempo porque puedes hacer otras cosas mientras la escuchas.
6 No comparto tu opinión porque a mi modo de ver es mejor ver lo que están explicando o comentando, sobre todo cuando es un documental o un partido de fútbol o de tenis.
7 Claro que sí pero la radio es muy útil si estás de viaje porque nunca te pierdes los resultados de los partidos. También puedes pasar el tiempo oyendo radionovelas o tertulias con entrevistas a gente del momento en tu emisora preferida.
8 También con la tele todos podemos aprender mucho si elegimos canales dedicados a la cultura o a la enseñanza. Los niños aprecian y comprenden las cosas mil veces mejor si hay algo visual con lo que pueden conectar las palabras.

Answers:

1 TV – *distrae, variedad*
2 radio – *te concentras más*
3 radio – *usas más imaginación*
4 radio – *tele es malo para los niños*
5 radio – *puedes hacer otra cosa*
6 TV – *hay que ver para seguir el comentario*
7 radio – *útil cuando estés de viaje*
8 TV – *cultura, enseñanza*

2b Students then write down three points in favour of first television and then radio.

This could follow a class discussion to enable students to form opinions and to gather useful vocabulary.

Técnica

Listening skills and taking notes while listening. (Take students through each point, discussing and commenting on them to gauge how competent and confident they already feel with listening tasks.) Use the transcript to show students how to focus on key language or vocabulary.

A Discuss with the students how they tackled activity 2a.

B Now help students prepare themselves for the listening task in activity 3.

 3 Students listen and classify the programmes. Since this vocabulary is already listed on page 19, they should be encouraged to complete the task from memory.

P 21, actividad 3

1 Mira, mira, mira, cómo está adelantando al otro ese fenómeno de chico. Nuestro Fernando Alonso está acelerando y va ganando. Les juro que nuestro campeón mundial va a subir al podio otra vez.

2 Estamos esperando, estamos esperando pero el tiempo pasa y los competidores están pensando, considerando su respuesta – ¿cuál va a ser? Nos preguntamos todos, pendientes de si acertarán o no … ay no, ¿qué están diciendo …?

3 Ahora está cantando y moviéndose al compás de la música. ¡Qué voz! ¡Qué letra! Nos entusiasma este joven que está irrumpiendo en la escena musical.

4 Está saliendo, sacando el hocico por el hueco, olfateando, mirando con mucho cuidado antes de sacar a las crías recién nacidas de su hogar.

5 Estamos presenciando un momento clave en el que estos dos líderes cruciales para la paz mundial se están saludando por primera vez tras una época escalofriante llena de tensiones – ahora están sentándose el uno junto al otro y parece que están hablando animadamente – a ver lo que está pasando …

Answers:

1 *retransmisión deportiva*

2 *concurso*

3 *programa de música*

4 *documental*

5 *telediario*

4 A group discussion. Students comment on the cartoon which should start a discussion about the pros and cons of TV.

5 This is a group activity. Students carry out a class survey about TV and radio preferences using the questions provided. Remind them about percentages and fractions when presenting the information, as supplied in the *frases clave.*

¿Telebasura o programas educativos?

Grammar focus

♦ The preterite tense using radical-changing verbs

♦ Synonyms and antonyms

Skills focus

♦ Listening skills continued

Key language

Estoy de acuerdo al cien por cien con …
Habéis dado en el clavo a la hora de decir que …
Me parece muy acertado …
Lo peor de todo es que …
Mi opinión es que …

Resources

♦ Students' Book pages 22 and 23

♦ CD 1, track 17

♦ Hoja 3

♦ Grammar Workbook page 40

1a Students listen to the opinions about reality TV and make notes. Remind them about the listening skills they discussed on the previous spread especially about anticipating language and vocabulary and also creating their own abbreviations.

P 22, actividad 1a

Preguntamos a 20 personas su opinión sobre los programas de telerrealidad – he aquí algunas de sus respuestas – a ver lo que opináis vosotros. ¿Son intrusivos o son inofensivos?

1 Ver esta clase de programas, sobre todo los programas rosa, me hace olvidarme de todos mis problemas – que tampoco son demasiado graves.

2 Pues yo creo que la gente joven de mi edad nos reímos bastante y no consideramos nada grave ver accidentes en vídeos domésticos, o a gente aireando sus miserias que acaba pegándose.

3 A mí me emocionan y no me importa que muestren escenas explícitas – me hacen reír y no me las tomo en serio.

4 Yo los considero morbosos y humillantes y no me gustan, pero en fin, sé que la mayoría de la gente disfruta con estos programas y no hay que tomárselos en serio.

5 Lo que pasa es que cuando alguien está describiendo lo que acaba de pasar en un accidente, por ejemplo, me pone la carne de gallina pero si estoy viendo tonterías en casa, me hace reír.

6 No tiene nada de nuevo – desde los romanos, la gente se ha divertido viendo sufrir al prójimo – piensa en los cristianos que se echaban a las fieras o los esclavos que luchaban por su libertad – sólo estamos presenciando las mismas escenas transformadas para el siglo XXI.

7 Digan lo que digan, al público le encanta ventilar sus problemas, sus deseos o ansiedades ya sea a través de la radio, la prensa o la tele. Ahora gracias al holandés John de Mol tenemos cámaras las 24 horas del día enfocadas en los concursantes de Gran hermano.

8 Muchas veces se exagera la realidad porque a la gente le entusiasma tener sus quince minutos de fama – harían lo que fuera para alcanzar la

---

fama y por eso no creo que haya que ser
demasiado crítico – déjales que se expresen a
su manera. La libertad de expresión es
imprescindible en una sociedad democrática y
libre.

1b Students read the statements and indicate
whether they agree or not with the notes they have
just taken.

Answers:

1 ✗ 2 ✓ 3 ✓ 4 *no se dice* 5 ✗ 6 ✓

1c Students listen a second time and make a list of
positive and then negative opinions.

1d Students use the *frases clave* to give their own
opinions about reality TV and discuss recent
examples – both good and bad – to illustrate. Remind
them they should always try to justify their opinions.

2a Students read the text quickly – once for gist and
then slightly more closely to make sure they have the
key words which they then use to make a brief oral
résumé in English.

2b Organise students into groups to discuss among
themselves how this compares with their own
experience.

2c Get students to use the *frases clave* to give their
own reactions to the text.

Gramática

The preterite tense continued – radical changes.

♦ Ensure students understand the term radical-
changing verbs, and then refer them to the
relevant grammar section of the Students' Book
and the Grammar Workbook.

♦ Remind them about radical-changing verbs in the
present tense as well.

♦ Students then complete tasks A and B.

Answers:

A 1 *sintió* **2** *pidieron* **3** *siguió* **4** *riñeron* **5** *prefirió*

B 1 *El héroe murió al final de la película.*

　　2 *Durmieron durante todo el telediario.*

　　3 *Como en todas las telenovelas el carácter /
　　protagonista principal mintió.*

　　4 *Se vistieron como personajes de los Simpsons.*

　　5 *Anoche repitieron mi programa favorito.*

3a Reading. Students read the two texts and
compare the main opinions. These are denser and
longer texts than they have probably met so far. This
gives an opportunity to illustrate that they do not
always have to translate word for word, but rather
gain an overall understanding of a text. The two texts

could be put side by side on an OHT or whiteboard
so that students follow visually with the differences
being highlighted in different colours. The Técnica
box on synonyms and antonyms could be discussed
prior to completing this task as it could help students
to exploit the vocabulary better.

On 23 Febuary, 1981, a group of Civil Guards took
the Congress and all the MPs in it hostage. Only
when the king, Juan Carlos, spoke over the radio
later that evening did the whole coup fail. It was the
fact that he was able to speak directly to the people
via the radio and later the television that defused
what could have been a disastrous situation.

3b Writing and speaking. Students note down the
arguments for and against. Exploit this further with
oral questions.

3c Then they answer the questions in full sentences.

Answers should include:

1 *basura en la tele*

2 *hay programas mejor o peor hechos*

3 *que la violencia siempre ha existido*

4 *Students answer in their own words. Following
class or pairwork discussion this could be used
as an essay topic.*

Técnica

Synonyms and antonyms.

This section could be exploited before tackling the
texts. The work should be familiar to students from
work covered in English lessons so ask for examples
in English first. Point out that not just nouns and
verbs have synonyms and antonyms but that various
other parts of speech do also and that it will help
them to write more interesting answers if they can
begin to spot these.

A 1 la violencia　　**2** el reflejo　　**3** inánime
　　4 investigar / registrar / buscar　**5** no obstante

B 1 gustan　　**2** la libertad　　**3** requerimos / damos
　　/ exigimos　**4** éxito　**5** sencillo

Continue using the texts as a basis for further
exploitation like this.

Anuncios y publicidad

Grammar focus

♦ The present subjunctive – formation and uses

♦ Verbs of wanting, requesting and advising

Skills focus

♦ Language of persuasion

Key language

- *Quiero que* + subjunctive
- *Espero que* + subjunctive
- *Insisto en que* + subjunctive
- *¿De qué trata? ¿Cuál es el tema?*

Resources

- Students' Book pages 24 and 25
- CD 1, track 18
- Hojas 2, 4
- Grammar Workbook pages 53, 55

Gramática

The present subjunctive – formation and uses.

- Allow plenty of time for students to discuss why the subjunctive is used in Spanish and how it affects the whole sentence. This allows a valuable opportunity for students to practise analytical skills on sentence structure and to apply their understanding of language and make comparisons between English and Spanish.

A 1 *c*   2 *d*   3 *b*   4 *a*

- Present the formation of the present subjunctive so that students fully appreciate the difference between the indicative and the subjunctive patterns.

A Students list the verbs in the subjunctive.

Answers:

1 *veas;* 2 *cambies;* 3 *escuchen;* 4 *grabe;* 5 *sigas;* 6 *acompañemos;* 7 *lea; ponga;* 8 *bajemos;* 9 *vaya;* 10 *critique*

B Students explain why the subjunctive is used, i.e. after verbs of wanting, requesting and advising.

C Students translate the sentences into English – orally.

1 I want you to watch the news at ten o'clock.
2 I insist you change channels.
3 We hope they will listen to the radio tonight.
4 He / she advises me to tape the documentary.
5 I don't want you to go on watching so much junk TV!
6 My sister needs us to go with her to the quiz show.
7 Do you want me to read the magazine to you or to put the TV on?
8 They ask us to lower the volume / turn the volume down.
9 My father won't allow me to go with you.
10 My brother can't stop me from criticising the programme.

Técnica

Language of persuasion.
Take students through the points one by one, commenting on them and discussing each of them. It would help to show advertisements in Spanish and English to illustrate the kind of language used.

A Students study the advertisement and complete the sentences using the verbs in the subjunctive supplied.

1 They then look at the advertisement again and prepare their own responses.

2a Students listen to the report and note down the information required. Ensure students study the questions before they listen and also anticipate language and vocabulary. They could also make some abbreviations to help them in their note taking. The transcript could be used after they have completed the task to show them where the answers lie.

P 25, actividad 2a

Hoy por hoy nadie puede negar que las campañas publicitarias tienden a influir nuestros hábitos de una u otra forma.
Piensa en las campañas navideñas que avisan de los peligros de conducir cuando sobrepasamos los límites de alcohol permitidos o las campañas dirigidas a la gente joven para decir no al tabaco o a las drogas. En efecto todas las campañas que tienen que ver con la salud o nos informan de peligros y riesgos influyen en nuestra manera de pensar.
Pero en Navidades también nos bombardean con otras campañas para comprar esto o lo otro, vestirnos con esta o aquella marca, beber o comer todos esos dulces que dañan los dientes o engordan. Nos provocan hasta que terminamos comprando lo que no necesitamos o lo que no nos conviene. Ni siquiera voy a tocar el tema de los anuncios aún más provocativos e incluso obscenos.
Por eso nos preguntamos: ¿Ha llegado el momento de reintroducir la censura? Estoy hablando específicamente de la censura que existía antes de 1966, que cambió con la Ley de Prensa en abril del mismo año y comenzó una actitud un poco más liberal y aun así hubo supresión de mucha información política.
¿Quién no se acuerda del "destape" cuando la desnudez llegó en 1977 con toda su gloria, belleza y pornografía? Basta con echar un vistazo a los quioscos de hoy para ver cantidades de revistas con anuncios picantes y casi pornográficos.

Answers:

1 *peligros de conducir con alcohol; decir no a las drogas*

2 *compras de Navidad; beber o comer cosas que engordan*

3 *supresión de información política*

4 *1966 la Ley de Prensa; 1977 el destape*

5 *persuadir; incitar a comprar*

6 *llamar la atención con imágenes seductoras, escalofriantes, imposibles o cómicas*

2b Students discuss the practicalities of censorship on advertising. They discuss the various techniques involved and give good and bad examples.

La prensa

Grammar focus
♦ Suffixes

Skills focus
♦ Different registers of language

Key language
♦ *semanal, quincenal, mensual, cotilleo*
♦ Slang words like *mogollón, me flipa, me mola*
♦ Suffixes ending in *-illo, -ito, -azo, -ón, -ucho, -uelo etc.*

Resources
♦ Students' Book pages 26 and 27
♦ CD 1, track 19
♦ Hoja 1

 1a Students listen to the discussion about different newspapers and magazines and identify them from the illustrated titles.

P 26, actividad 1a

1 Yo leo todos los días *El País* porque me informa bien sobre lo que está pasando, no sólo en España sino en todo el mundo. Me parece que es un periódico bastante objetivo y neutral en su opinión política y que te enseña a considerar varios puntos de vista.

2 Si es por la opinión política yo escojo *Cambio 16* porque informa y opina pero siempre con buen sentido del humor y yo creo que esto es esencial hoy en día. Además nunca me canso de una buena sátira de vez en cuando porque los políticos se toman a sí mismos muy en serio y es refrescante leer algo que les critica cada semana.

3 Uf, yo no puedo con tanta seriedad – para mí lo mejor de cada día es leer el *Marca* – ése sí es un periódico que vale la pena leer de pe a pa – todo lo que se necesita saber del deporte está ahí cada día, y no creas que es frívolo – nada de eso – nosotros tomamos muy en serio el deporte y con razón *Marca* es el periódico más leído de España.

4 Pues yo considero que no hay cosa más fascinante que leer todo sobre la vida de las estrellas de cine y de la sociedad. Pueden decir lo que quieran, que es prensa de cotilleo o de corazón, pero es lo único que a mí me interesa de verdad – cada semana me entero de todo, en *¡Hola!* por supuesto.

5 Prefiero *Semana* porque, como se deduce de su título, sale cada semana y contiene un poco de todo – chismes de sociedad, programación de la televisión y no deja de incluir artículos sobre el mundo de la moda – todo lo que a mí me fascina.

6 Los artículos de *Muy Interesante* tratan de informar, educar y entretener a la vez y es por eso que la compro cada mes – siempre hay reportajes serios y a veces, como en *Quo*, hay artículos originales de interés general.

7 Nosotros los Superpoperos estamos todos de acuerdo en que la única revista que atiende a nuestros gustos es *Super Pop*. Cada quince días quedamos para comprarla y compartirla.

8 Pues yo no comprendo por qué sigo comprando *Interviú* porque a veces lo encuentro demasiado picante y obsceno; sin embargo, lo compro cada semana porque también presenta los reportajes de una manera distinta.

1b Students then classify the different titles.

Answers:

El País: diario – gran formato
Cambio 16: semanal – noticias
Marca: diario – deporte
¡Hola!: semanal – cotilleo
Semana: semanal – cotilleo – moda
Muy Interesante: mensual – interés general
Quo: mensual – interés general
Super Pop: quincenal – pop
Interviú: semanal – cotilleo – interés general – noticias
Deia: diario
El Mundo: diario
La Vanguardia: diario
ABC: diario
Bravo: quincenal – moda – pop

1c Encourage students to research more titles and their content on line. Bring in as many magazines and papers as possible so that they appreciate the different styles.

1d In pairs, get students to discuss what they read at home and how it compares with what they can read in Spain.

2 Point out to students that word derivations are a useful way to avoid using a dictionary – students should begin to group words of similar roots.

Sample answers:

1 *redactor* 2 *titular* 3 *periodista*
4 *lectura* 5 *editor* 6 *reportero*

3 Students begin to recognise the different styles of headlines and classify them.

Sample answers:

a   *Ingeniería tamaño microchip*
b   *Loco por el Barça*
c   *amores, mentiras y !grandes sorpresas!*
d   *Los mejores desnudos del verano – poster*

Técnica

Different registers of language.
Take students through the points raised and ask for their reactions and comments. They should provide examples of their own to make sure they have a clear idea about the term 'registers of language'.

A Students classify programmes they have watched or heard recently.

B Students discuss headlines.

C Students name a newspaper, magazine or programme that can be best described by each adjective.

D Students say where they expect to see or hear the vocabulary.

4 Reading. Students read the text and answer the questions in their own words.

Answers should include:

1 *de la falta de privacidad*
2 *entre la policía y los periodistas*
3 *vago*

5 Students compare the two different ways of reporting the same topic. Choose more recent examples about a topical event and ask students to match them and then comment on the styles of reporting.

Answers:

1 *A1 más serio; A2 salaz*
2 *Hechizan is an example of the type of verb used.*
3 *A1*
4 *Students answer for themselves and justify their answers.*

Gramática

Suffixes.
Ensure students understand the terms diminutive, augmentative and pejorative. Ask for examples in English and then see how many words they already know that have suffixes in Spanish. This could be done as a whole class exercise to make a comprehensive list. They could also discuss how suffixes are used in advertising to add to the shade of meaning desired.

B

Answers:

1 *casita, casilla, casona, casucha*
2 *chiquillo, chiquito*
3 *maletica, maletón*
4 *ojitos, ojones, ojazos,*
5 *papelito, papelón, papelucho.*

Gramática en acción

Resources

♦ Students' Book page 28
These sections can be used to revise and reinforce new grammar structures or to test out how much students have retained from the unit.

Negatives

Students should revise page 19 and also the relevant grammar sections.

A Ask students to copy the sentences and complete them with an appropriate negative.

Answers:

1 *ninguna – ningún*
2 *ninguna*
3 *nunca*
4 *tampoco*
5 *nadie*
6 *nada que*

B Students translate the sentences as required.

Answers:

1 Not even sports interest me. / I'm not even interested in sport.
2 Has anyone sent the remote control ? No one has.
3 They never put anything on that I like.
4 No political debate interests me on the news.
5 *Nada ha cambiado entonces. / No ha cambiado nada entonces.*
6 *Nunca te han gustado las noticias, ¿verdad?*
7 *Ni siquiera las pusiste.*
8 *Ni las noticias ni los documentales.*

C Students make up sentences of their own using five different negatives.

Verbs + infinitive

Refer students to the relevant grammar section. Students will begin to show just how well they are coping with language structures when they master the difference between English and Spanish constructions using two verbs when English uses a present participle – 'I like listening to the radio' and Spanish a verb plus the infinitive – *me gusta escuchar la radio*. This will be even more evident once they can recognise when to use a subjunctive.

D

Answers:

List a) = *le gusta; prefieren; quieres; puedes; me encanta*

List b) = *relajarse; escuchar; poner; cambiar; ver*

E

1 *He/she likes to relax by watching sports programmes.*
2 *They prefer to listen to the radio.*
3 *Do you want to put on another radio station.*
4 *You can change the channel if you want.*
5 *I love watching documentaries about animals.*

A escoger

Resources

♦ Students' Book page 29
♦ CD 1, track 20

1a Students listen to the extracts and classify them.

> P 29, actividad 1a
>
> 1 Con su apoteósico triunfo en Hungría, donde consiguió doblar a Michael Schuhmacher, Fernando Alonso ha hecho historia – es el piloto más joven que sube a lo más alto del podio en Fórmula 1 y el primer español que logra tal proeza.
> 2 Cóctel de noticias – aunque mi disco se llama *Locura* soy muy tranquilita, nos confesó ayer la joven tras declarar que ya no sigue saliendo con …
> 3 Olvide la dieta libre de grasas, nunca conseguirá estar más delgado que nuestro DVD – equipo DVD Home Cinema: el sistema más plano del mundo.
> 4 Hoy el primer ministro español viaja a Londres donde se encontrará con su colega, el primer ministro británico, para intercambiar sus opiniones sobre …
> 5 Esta tarde se preven cielos poco nubosos, con intervalos soleados pero con posibilidad de chubascos tormentosos dispersos, más

> probables en las zonas de la sierra y en la zona del Estrecho.

Answers:
1 *deportivo*
2 *chisme / cotilleo*
3 *propaganda*
4 *informativo*
5 *pronóstico del tiempo*

1b Students listen a second time and this time they add two more pieces of information for each extract.

Answers:
1 *piloto más joven; primer español a ganar el Fórmula 1.*
2 *su disco se llama Locura; ya no sale con X.*
3 Home Cinema *– un sistema muy plano*
4 *el primer ministro español viaja a Londres a hablar con el primer ministro británico*
5 *cielos poco nubosos, intervalos soleados*

2 Students read the two texts about war and answer the questions in their own words. They comment on the register of language used.

3 Students read the statements about the media and decide which are favourable and which are not.

Answers:

1 × 2 ✓ 3 ✓ 4 × 5 ✓ 6 × 7 × 8 ✓

4 Students use the strapline and make up their own advertisement / campaign.

5 Students read the information about newscasts in Spain and then carry out a quick opinion poll by noting the answers to the questions and then comparing their findings with the rest of the class. This could serve as a basis for an essay at a later stage.

6 Students prepare their ideas about the benefits and future of television and then present them to the class.

Unidad 2 La generación conectada

Unit objectives
By the end of this unit students will be able to:
- Describe and comment on examples of new technology
- Discuss reasons for adopting new technology
- Talk about internet usage and 'rules'
- Decide whether technology is changing today's society

Grammar
By the end of this unit students will be able to:
- Use *se* to avoid the passive voice
- Use irregular verbs in the preterite
- identify verbs followed by the infinitive and by a preposition
- Use the imperative
- Recognise the use of the subjunctive for wanting / not wanting things to happen
- Recognise the use of the subjunctive for value judgements and emotions

Skills
By the end of this unit students will be able to:
- employ different strategies for reading

Resources
- Students' Book pages 30 and 31
- CD 1, track 21

1 By way of an introduction to the unit, students read the descriptions and match them to the objects displayed.

Answers:
1 *C*   2 *A*   3 *E*   4 *B*   5 *D*

 2 Students listen to the recording and identify which object is being spoken about. They listen also for an opinion about each object.

P 31, actividad 2

1 Acabo de comprarlo, así que todavía no lo he utilizado, pero me imagino que va a ser muy divertido. No tendré que gritar, y espero que a Tufo también le guste.

2 Es exactamente lo que necesito. A la moda pero a la vez práctico. Voy a poder ahorrar tiempo, dinero y electricidad.

3 Es feo y ridículo. No quiero hablar con un monigote así de tonto. Se lo voy a regalar a mi hermano. Le va a parecer muy simpático.

---

4 Pensé que era una broma. No puede existir una cosa tan inútil, o si existe, no han de vender muchos. Ni siquiera tiene memoria. ¿Quién necesita desodorante para su ordenador?

5 No. No va a funcionar. Si descuelgas el auricular, se te va a caer el móvil al suelo.

Answers:
1 *remote control wireless dog device – amusing*
2 *solar powered handbag   fashionable and practical*
3 *skype phone monster – ugly and ridiculous*
4 *USB airwick – a joke, who needs it?*
5 *retro handset for mobile – won't work*

Gramática

Using *se* to avoid the passive.

Remind students about the form and purpose of this structure. In exercise A ask them to identify all the sentences which use *se* this on the page. They should do two versions of a translation of each example (as in the example): first a literal version, then one in correct English.

3 Individually students prepare a presentation. They choose one of the objects as if they were promoting it. The class / group then votes on which object is the most convincing.

4 Students invent an object of their own, and then write a description of it using the passive grammar structure with *se*.

La tecnología está de moda

Grammar focus
- Irregular preterite verbs
- Verbs + infinitive or followed by a preposition

Skills focus
- Reading strategies

Key language
- *di dije estuve fui hice pude puse quise supe traje tuve vi acabar con acabar de comenzar a   consistir en*   plus similar verbs

Resources
- Students' Book pages 32 and 33
- CD 1, tracks 22–23

♦ Hojas 6, 7, 10
♦ Grammar workbook pages 40, 65

1 Students read the text and decide which of the four sentences are true or false. (Verdad or Mentira)

Answers:
1 M   2 M   3 V   4 V

2a Students listen and decide which of the two people is speaking; the sales rep or JMLH.

P 32, actividad 2a

1 Es importante proteger la propiedad intelectual de los artistas. Las nuevas tecnologías hacen que sea más fácil comprar música, pero también que sea más fácil copiarla y robarla. Queremos que los artistas reciban el dinero que merecen, y no podemos permitir que se hagan copias ilegales para compartir o vender.

2 La nueva tecnología acaba con el monopolio de las grandes compañías. A ellas no les importa la música, sólo el márketing y el dinero. Internet es más democrático. La música ya no es un disco, un objeto que se vende … es algo efímero, como la música en vivo o en la radio. Se escucha, se aprecia, y siempre existe la posibilidad de escuchar más música … incluso música alternativa que nunca tuvo su oportunidad con los grandes sellos …

Answers:
1 *representante de la compañía*
2 JMLH

2b Students listen a second time and note down the ideas. They use these as a basis for a discussion.

Gramática

♦ Irregular preterite verbs

You can present these either as new grammar, or as revision, depending on the stage of learning of the students.

A Students check the preterite form of each verb and give the infinitive.

B Students translate the sentences.

Answers:
1 *Dijo que no es ilegal.*
2 *Puso la música en una página web.*
3 *Lo hizo pero no por dinero.*
4 *No podían probar / pudieron comprobar que vendía la música.*
5 *Tuvieron que aceptar lo que dijo el juez.*

3 Students read the descriptions and decide which of the photos is being described.

Answers:
1 C   2 A   3 B

4 Students listen and choose a piece of equipment for Raúl, Jesús and Celia.

P 33, actividad 4

Raúl
Pensaba comprar un MP3 porque quería escuchar música mientras me dedicaba a hacer deporte, pero decidí comprar uno que puedo utilizar también como teléfono.

Celia
A los 46 años, no voy a empezar a jugar a videojuegos, pero tengo ganas de comprar un aparato para poder escuchar música y con una pantalla lo suficientemente grande como para ver fotos y vídeos.

Jesús
No voy a volver a comprar otro aparato. Acabo de encontrar éste que incluye todo lo que quiero. Me puedo conectar a Internet, tiene juegos excelentes, y admite 300 canciones o mil fotos de alta resolución.

Answers:
Raúl A; Jesús B; Celia C

5 Students look for more examples of technical words for ICT, using the *frases clave* as a guide.

Gramática

Verbs + a preposition and an infinitive. Students need to learn these constructions by heart.

A Students organise the list of verbs according to what follows them.

Answers:

B
comprar; escuchar; a hacer; comprar; utilizar; empezar; jugar; comprar; poder; escuchar; ver; volver; comprar; encontrar; conectar

C
pensaba; quería; me dedicaba a; decidí; puedo; voy a; tengo genas de; voy a; acabo de; me puedo

6 Students talk about their own gadgets.

La blogosfera

Grammar focus

♦ Imperatives – positive, negative, with *usted* and *ustedes*
♦ Subjunctive with wanting / not wanting things to happen

Key language

♦ *levanta levantad; abre abrid; No hagas eso. Ayude al señor, por favor.*

♦ *un bloguero los newbies los chaters un friki los troles*

Resources

♦ Students' Book pages 34 and 35
♦ CD 1, track 24
♦ Grammar Workbook pages 55, 60
♦ Hoja 6

1 Students choose definitions for the ICT vocabulary.

Answers:

a *los newbies*

b *un friki*

c *un bloguero*

d *los chaters*

e *los usuarios títeres*

f *los troles*

2 Students listen and check on each definition.

P 34, actividad 2

a Los **newbies** molestan a los usuarios habituales, no porque quieran provocar problemas, sino porque ignoran las reglas y hacen preguntas tontas.

b Soy un **friki**. Lo que más me gusta son los ordenadores e Internet. También me gustan los videojuegos, y paso mucho tiempo jugando.

c Soy un **bloguero**. Tengo un blog personal donde doy mis opiniones sobre el mundo. Blog es una palabra que viene del inglés y significa web log, que es como una bitácora o diario personal.

d Soy un **chater**. Me gusta mandar mensajes SMS y es más rápido y corto escribir las palabras a mi manera.

e Yo manejo varios **usuarios títeres**. Tengo dos o tres nombres diferentes en Internet y nadie sabe mi nombre real.

f Yo creo que los blogs son tonterías. A veces me aburro y pongo mensajes abusivos en los blogs para divertirme. ¡Dicen que soy un **trol**!

Gramática

Imperatives.

Students will already be familiar with the imperative form but now need to fully understand how to form it and which form to use when.

A Students find examples of positive forms and explain how each one is formed.

Answers:

5 *Respeta la ortografía del idioma castellano aportar comentarios relevantes.*

7 *Trata de al debate aportar comentarios relevantes*

10 *Respeta a los otros usuarios aportar comentarios relevantes*

B Students do the same for all the negative imperatives.

Answers:

1 *No contravengas el Código Penal de España.*
Explanation: neg = subjunctive 1st person present tense of *venir = vengo.* ar endings 2nd person: *vengas*

2 *No hagas comentarios abusivos*
Explanation: neg = subjunctive.1st person present tense of *hacer = hago.* ar endings 2nd person: *hagas*

3 *No utilices palabras malsonantes.*
Explanation: neg = subjunctive. *utilizar* 1st person = *utilizo* but the spelling changes: *a* becomes *e.* er endings 2nd person: *utilices*

4 *No escribas en mayúsculas.*
Explanation: neg = subjunctive. *escribir* 1st person present = *escribo.* ar endings 2nd person: *escribas*

6 *No pongas vínculos a de SPAM páginas*
Explanation: neg = use of the subjunctive: *poner* 1st person present = *pongo pongas*

8 *No difundas información falsa.*
Explanation: neg = the subjunctive

9 *No inventes identidades alternativas*
Explanation: neg = subjunctive

C Students write out the rules in Spanish.

Answers:

1 *No borres los ficheros en el disco duro derrames.*

2 *No té en el teclado.*

3 *Lleva tus bagels en cajas de CDs.*

3 Students read the rules for blogs 1–10 and then match the sentences a–g to each one.

Answers:

1 *a*   **2** *c*   **3** *g*   **4** *d*   **5** *b*   **6** *f*   **8** *e*

Gramática

The subjunctive: wanting / not wanting things to happen.
Revise the use and formation of the subjunctive from Unit 1. Ask students to explain what they think is meant by wanting things to happen and not happen and to give you examples in English. They should then analyse how to put their examples into Spanish.

A Students find examples of subjunctives in activity 4.

Answers:

1 *se llene;* **2** *sean;* **3** *participen;* **4** *se ofenda;*
5 *sea*

B Students work out the meanings of the sections in bold.

Answers:

1 *to stop;* **2** *to make sure that;* **3** *to allow;*
4 *so that / in order that;* **5** *to make sure that*

4 Students complete the sentences 1–5, using the phrases given in the blog rules, following the example given.

Example answers:

1 *Se prohíbe poner enlaces a sitios basura ... para* **impedir que** *el sitio se llene de contenidos basura.*
2 *Respeta la ortografía del idioma castellano ... para* **asegurar que** *los mensajes sean legibles.*
3 *Respeta a los otros usuarios ... para* **permitir que** *todos participen.*
4 *No hagas comentarios ofensivos ...* **para que** *los otros usuarios no se ofendan.*
5 *Trata de ser siempre relevante al debate ... para* **asegurar que** *tu texto sea coherente.*

5 Students invent a questionnaire to find out what types of ICT user their fellow students are.

6 In pairs, students answer the questions given.

Tecnología: los hechos

Grammar focus

♦ The subjunctive for value judgements and emotions

Key language

♦ *es importante que ...*
♦ *es ridículo que ...*
♦ *me fascina que ...*
♦ *es escandaloso que ...*
♦ *me sorprende que ...*
♦ *es una lástima que ...*

Resources

♦ Students' Book pages 36 and 37
♦ CD 1, track 25
♦ Hojas 8, 9
♦ Grammar Workbook page 56

1 Students read the text and complete the sentences using their own words. They should follow the example given.

Possible answers:

2 *El 62% de los jóvenes ... se conecta al Internet a diario.*
3 *Las chicas ... valoran Internet más para los estudios.*

4 *Los chicos ... tienen otras prioridades.*
5 *El "chat" ... es muy popular entre los jóvenes para comunicarse.*
6 *Las compras en Internet ... no son tan importantes como otros aspectos.*
7 *Las llamadas telefónicas ... son menos importantes que los SMS.*

Gramática

The subjunctive for value judgements and emotions.

This follows on from the work covered on the previous spread about the use of the subjunctive.

A Students could read through the four examples given here and then make further examples of their own, making sure they can explain what is meant by emotions and value judgements. Students should then give their own translations of the phrases in English.

2 Students use the *frases clave* to give their own opinions about the results of the survey from the previous page. They follow the example given.

3 Students read the statements 1–5. They decide whether they agree or not, and then give their own opinions. This is a reading and speaking exercise, not a grammar one, so they do not necessarily need to use the subjunctive in their answers. It should give them an opportunity to see some more examples.

 4 Students listen to Raquel, Ngozi and Marco and make notes. They then answer the question about how typical these opinions are for young Spaniards according to the survey.

P 37, actividad 4

Raquel
Necesito pasar varias horas al día delante de la pantalla de mi ordenador para descargar música para mi iPod. También tengo muchos amigos en varios chats y tengo que comunicarme con ellos a diario. No utilizo el móvil porque sólo conozco a mis amigos por Internet.

Ngozi
No tengo mucha experiencia con los ordenadores. No tengo ordenador en mi casa, y en las clases de informática prefiero jugar a juegos online. Tengo un móvil, y suelo enviar muchos mensajes a mis amigos. Escucho música pero en mi lector de CDs.

Marco
Paso varias horas al día navegando por Internet. En las clases descargo ficheros de MP3 cuando los profesores no me miran, y por la tarde, en lugar de hacer mis deberes, prefiero enviar emails a mis amigos. También busco cosas para comprar, pero no compro por Internet, sino que investigo el mejor precio y luego lo compro en una tienda.

Answers:

Marco – Yes, pretty typical Spanish boy

Ngozi – Not too typical – text messages, yes. Video games more popular with boys than girls. Still listens to CDs –behind the times.

Raquel – Chats (typical) music fairly typical. Mobile phone not typical.

5 Students use the *frases clave* to write their opinions of the three young people.

Tecnología y sociedad

Grammar focus

♦ Consolidation of previous grammar presented in the unit

Skills focus

♦ Reading strategies

Key language

♦ *el aislamiento*
♦ *la invasión de la privacidad*
♦ *apoderarse de*
♦ *imponer*
♦ *Caperucita*
♦ *lobo*
♦ + all *frases clave*

Resources

♦ Students' Book pages 38 and 39
♦ CD 1, tracks 26–27
♦ Hoja 10

Técnica

♦ Reading strategies

A After reading the list of reading strategies, discuss each of its points with the students and ask for their comments. They should then decide which are the most effective for themselves and which for the whole class.

¡Menos logos, Caperucita!

Cultural note: The expression is '*Menos lobos Caperucita*' meaning 'not so many wolves, Red Riding Hood', or 'Don't cry wolf' (this is a direct link with the text – because the supposed dangers didn't materialize), but making a pun with 'logos', as the text also refers to the demise of big bad brands! Note the link to the cartoon.

a There are no numbers, and the people / places are not proper nouns, although there are some there. The point is that even if you don't find any, you have combed through the text once while looking for them.

b The title and the picture help you anticipate word play / tough ideas / playful ideas, but they don't help you.

c There are lots of cognates, but finding specific ones is again less important than the process of a third reading through of the text.

d There is a list prefaced by a colon in the first paragraph. While students were looking for questions, they may have found the initials 'SMS' and added that strategy to their list.

e This is probably the most useful, as there are lots of sentence starters or sentence halves.

f This is quite useful too because more sophisticated strategies have to come into play, as you could have predicted, given the opaque nature of the title and picture. This leads on to point 'g' which is another warning.

Now students are familiar with the text and aware of its difficulty, they are ready to tackle factual questions on the points that are less opaque.

1 Students read the text and decide which of the 10 statements given below are a reality, which a possibility, and which are not a reality, according to what they have read.

Answers:

1 *Realidad*
2 *No se ha hecho realidad*
3 *No se ha hecho realidad*
4 *No se ha hecho realidad*
5 *Es una realidad*
6 *Es una realidad*
7 *Es una realidad*
8 *Es una posibilidad*
9 *Es una realidad*
10 *Es una realidad*

 2a Students listen and decide which of the statements 1–5 are true or false.

P 39, actividad 2a

– ¿Son perjudiciales los videojuegos?
– Típicamente los jóvenes que juegan en exceso también demuestran síntomas sociales tales como mal rendimiento escolar, aislamiento. Sin embargo, para los menos extrovertidos, pueden mejorar su autoestima. Además pueda ayudar la coordinación. Por eso, pensamos que jugar con videojuegos puede ser bueno, siempre que se haga en su justa medida.
– ¿Cuál puede ser esa justa medida?
– No la puedo definir, pero podría ser una media hora diaria, aunque hay unos jóvenes que suelen pasar varias horas jugando.
– ¿Es cierto que puede ocasionar enfermedades?

– Pues, la estimulación por la luz de la pantalla puede provocar una crisis epiléptica. También los juegos violentos o machistas pueden producir problemas emocionales. Pero son casos aislados. Una preocupación más común es cuando el niño es incapaz de limitar el tiempo que se pasa jugando. Además de malgastar su tiempo, fomenta su adicción al juego.

Answers:

1 *M*   2 *M*   3 *V*   4 *V*   5 *V*

2b Students match up the two halves of the seven sentences according to what they have heard.

Answers:

1 *g*   2 *f*   3 *d*   4 *b*   5 *e*   6 *c*   7 *a*

3 Students work with a partner and answer the questions, using their own words and their own ideas.

4 Students listen to Rebeca and Luke answering one of the questions. Students should evaluate their responses. Use the *frases clave* to help form good sentences.

P 39, actividad 4

– ¿Cuál es la tecnología más importante para los jóvenes?
– Pues, yo diría ... personalmente que es ... el teléfono móvil porque siempre tengo el mío en el bolso. Lo utilizo para llamar a mis amigos, pero no en clase, claro ... los profesores no nos dejan que tengamos teléfonos ... también para mandar mensajes ... Mi agenda también está en el móvil y mis fotos. El teléfono también es un reproductor MP3, pero no sé utilizarlo ... Tengo un iPod y prefiero utilizar eso para escuchar música. Jugar a videojuegos en el teléfono, creo que eso tiene más importancia para los chicos. Sí, tendría que ser mi móvil.
– ¿La tecnología mejora la calidad de vida?
– Se podría decir que hoy la tecnología es menos importante que antes: que es para jugar, para comunicarse, para divertirse. No se trata de salvar la vida a los enfermos o educar a los niños. Pero son tecnologías que realmente tienen influencia en nuestra vida. Son aparatos que utilizamos cada día, sin pensarlo tal vez, pero que nos hacen la vida más fácil o más agradable.

5 Students reorganise the statements to form a basis for an essay and respond to the question about technology dominating our lives today. The teacher should specify the length. A possible plan could be as follows:

Introduction
Some of the pointless inventions from the opening spread, leading to restating the question

FOR
♦ expensive phones etc.
♦ predicted problems of the internet

AGAINST
♦ some positive results of technology
♦ the survey results showing it's not happened
♦ young people's attitudes + intelligent use of technology, communication, awareness of own purchasing power, end of music as a commodity, own language, knowledge of world, make own use of technology, set demands on companies

Gramática en acción

Resources
♦ Students' Book page 40

A Students read and match up the two halves of the sentences 1–7.

Possible answers:

1 *e*   2 *a*   3 *b*   4 *f*   5 *c*   6 *g*   7 *d*

B Students write their own sentences about security.

C Students revise the reminder box and then fill in the form, deciding why the subjunctive is being used in sentences 1–5.

Answers:

1 wanting
2 wanting
3 value judgement / emotion
4 emotion
5 not wanting

D Students complete the sentences using a verb in the subjunctive.

Point out that the answers can be given in the *tú* form, but don't have to be, except for 4.

Answers:

1 (*comprar*) *compres*
2 (*saber*) *sepas*
3 (*enviar*) *envies*
4 (*poner*) *pongas*
5 (*gastar*) *gastes*
6 (*ser*) *sea*
7 (*pasar*) *pases*

A escoger

Resources
♦ Students' Book page 41
♦ CD 1, track 28

1 Students listen to Erica and decide if the statements that follow are true, false or not made, according to the recording.

> **P 41, actividad 1**
>
> Quería empezar a salir otra vez después de la muerte de mi primer esposo, y me inscribí en una agencia en Internet. Buscaba a alguien serio, pero con buen sentido del humor también. Así conocí a Juan Manuel. Hablamos por teléfono y salimos a comer los dos. La primera vez que le presenté a Juan Manuel a mi familia fue en Navidad. Ya habíamos decidido vivir juntos ... entonces nos casamos.
>
> Los dos teníamos hijos y nietos, y queríamos integrar las dos familias. Todos estaban de acuerdo.
>
> Para mis nietos Juan Manuel es su abuelo. Lo admiran, y él mima a los más jóvenes: se pelean por sentarse a su lado en la mesa. Le llaman "abuelito", aunque mlde un metro 90.
>
> En casa fue bastante fácil acomodarnos el uno al otro. Como mi marido se acostumbró a vivir solo, sabe cuando hay que lavar la ropa, sabe cocinar – muy bien, pero suele cocinar lo que a él le gusta, sin contar las calorías, ni el colesterol.

Answers:

1 *V* **2** *V* **3** *F* **4** *NSD* **5** *F* **6** *F* **7** *F* **8** *F*

2 Students complete the test and decide if they have *movilitis* – i.e. if they are addicted to mobiles.

3 Students read the text and write answers to questions 1–5, using their own words.

4 Students read the statements and say if they agree with them or not, and why.

Repaso Unidades 1–2

Skills
Focus on listening and reading skills.

Resources
♦ Students' Book pages 42 and 43
♦ CD 1, tracks 29 and 30

1 Students read the text about the future of television and answer the questions.

Answers:

1 *la programación tradicional*

2 *Podremos elegir de entre un banco digital de programas*

3 *ver tele en una pantella plasma enorme, en el móvil o en el ordenador portátil*

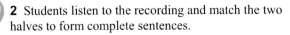

2 Students listen to the recording and match the two halves to form complete sentences.

Answers:

1 *h* **2** *c* **3** *f* **4** *g* **5** *b* **6** *a* **7** *e* **8** *d*

> **P 42, actividad 2**
>
> **1** Estoy de acuerdo con lo que dicen de los reporteros, porque me parece que a los periodistas no les importa torcer la verdad y escribir lo que les da la gana.
> **2** Habéis dado en el clavo a la hora de decir que ya nadie respeta a nadie – los momentos privados ya no existen. Sin embargo hay periódicos serios como *El País* que nos ayudan a apreciar lo que pasa en el mundo.
> **3** Me parece muy acertado cuando se dice que manipulan a la gente para que inventen escándalos sólo para tener sus quince minutos de fama.
> **4** Lo más vergonzoso de todo es que esta clase de reporteros parecen insensibles a la crítica de que carecen de moral. A mí me encanta la sátira de *Cambio 16* porque te enseña a reírte de ti mismo y de las noticias de actualidad.
> **5** En mi opinión, hay unos cuantos periodistas que son perezosos a morir y que no se esfuerzan por encontrar una buena historia.
> **6** Claro, y ¡*Hola!* está llena de cotilleos y no para de hablar de las estrellas y los famosos.

3 Students read the text about the inventor/invention of the smiley and complete the sentences in their own words, but basing their information on the text.

4 Students listen to the recording and note only the positive points of view.

Answers:

Con el móvil te mentienes en contacto; Internet te ayuda con los deberes; puedo hablar a larga distancia cuando quiera y es barato; tuve con quien hablar cuando me estaban amenazando en el cole; puedo trabajar desde casa o en el extranjero; puedes hacer mil cosas

> **P 43, actividad 4a**
>
> **1** A mi modo de ver, las ventajas son más evidentes que las desventajas; por ejemplo con el móvil te mantienes en contacto con tu familia todo el día si quieres e Internet te ayuda con los deberes.
> **2** No comparto tu opinión porque ya no es posible escapar ni de la gente ni del trabajo y eso me preocupa mucho. Te pueden contactar dondequiera que estés con mensajes o problemas y te sientes obligado a responder al instante y todo esto te causa cada vez más estrés.
> **3** En cuanto a mí, yo estoy contentísima porque puedo hablar a larga distancia cuando quiera y es muy barato. Imagina, hace sólo 20 años tenía que reservar hora para llamar a Colombia y ahora sólo tengo que marcar el número y tengo a mi gente al otro lado y por si fuera poco

cuando tenga el nuevo modelo podré verles
también.

4 Yo creo que es una cosa buenísima porque
cuando me estaban amenazando en el cole
pude llamar al 900 20 20 10 y enseguida tuve
con quien hablar, me dieron consejo y me
consolaron.

5 Los jóvenes pasan todo el día pegados al móvil
o al ordenador y eso no puede ser bueno ni para
los ojos ni para los oídos, ni tampoco para los
dedos, con tanto teclear.

6 Y el lenguaje que han inventado es
incomprensible – ya no se respeta la gramática
y ni el castellano puro que se hablaba en mis
tiempos.

7 Yo por lo menos estoy muy agradecida porque
significa que puedo trabajar desde casa o
incluso en el extranjero si quiero y me parece
que es un beneficio enorme.

8 Y parece mentira pero puedes hacer mil cosas
por Internet – hacer compras y operaciones
bancarias, reservar billetes de avión o tren y
hasta comprar entradas para ir al cine.

9 Me encanta porque te permite la interacción con
tus programas favoritos de la tele o de la radio.

4b Students listen a second time and choose the
answer which best fits each sentence.

Answers:

1 a   2 d   3 a   4 d

5 Students read the text and answer the questions.

Answers:

1 *ordenador, datos, informáticos, discos duros,
gigabytes, correo personal, borrar*

2 *Students' own suggestions*

3 *Mucha información puede extraerse fácilmente de
ordenadores después de venderlos.*

6a Students read the text and find equivalent
phrases.

Answers:

1 *sólo hace falta*

2 *que ... no se descuelgue*

3 *es un nuevo desafío*

4 *descargan algunas canciones*

5 *concienciarles*

6 *no han surtido efecto*

7 *tampoco ha dado resultado*

8 *en torno a*

9 *a la cola de*

10 *la alfabetización digital*

6b Students work in pairs and discuss the theme of
copyright and then make an oral presentation.

6c They then continue the discussion about how
things have changed and will continue to change
regarding copyright.

7 Students make two lists: one in favour of texting
and the other against.

Unidad 3 Foro de cultura popular

Unit objectives

By the end of this unit students will be able to:

♦ Discuss and write about all kinds of films, directors and actors
♦ Discuss and write about different types of theatre
♦ Discuss and write about famous musicians and their styles

Grammar

By the end of this unit students will be able to:

♦ Use written accents correctly
♦ Use the imperfect tense correctly
♦ Use object pronouns (both direct and indirect) correctly
♦ Use the pluperfect tense correctly
♦ Recognise and use a mixture of past tenses and understand how to sequence them
♦ Use *lo* and *lo que* correctly

Skills

By the end of this unit students will be able to:

♦ Put forward opinions and beliefs; agree and disagree
♦ Speak from notes
♦ Understand how to approach speaking stimulus material

Resources

♦ Students' Book pages 44 and 45
♦ CD 1, tracks 31–33

1a Students look at the name tags and see how many names they can recognise / identify. They link the names to the correct descriptions.

Answers: 1 *A*   2 *B*   3 *F*   4 *E*   5 *C*   6 *D*

1b Students research more names and write similar brief descriptions. This could be turned into a guessing game in pairs or as a whole class. Put the names into an envelope and each student picks a name out of the envelope and then has to match it to a description.

2a Students study and discuss the film poster.

 2b They then listen to the first dialogue and fill in the gaps.

P 45, actividad 2b

– ¿Qué tipo de cinéfilo eres? ¿Qué género prefieres?
– Pues, me encantan las aventuras y películas de fantasía con efectos especiales como Piratas del Caribe.
– ¿Quién es el director?

– Gore Verbinsky, pero no sé quién escribió el guión.
– ¿Quiénes son los intérpretes?
– Johnny Depp, Keira Knightly y Orlando Bloom son los protagonistas.
– Vale. ¿Y el argumento?
– Bueno, trata de las aventuras del capitán Sparrow ...

2c They adapt and practise the dialogue with a partner.

 2d They listen to further dialogues, noting down the information required.

P 45, actividad 2d

1
– ¿Qué tipo de película prefieres?
– Me encantan las comedias. ¿Y a ti?
– Prefiero las películas de fantasía con efectos especiales como *El Señor de los Anillos o Spiderman.*
– Sí, son impactantes, pero a veces son muy extravagantes. Lo que más me gusta son las películas que tratan de la vida normal como *Dame diez razones,* ya sean tristes, románticas o realistas.
– ¿Quién la dirigió?
– Creo que el director se llama Brad Silberling.
– ¿Quiénes son los protagonistas?
– Morgan Freeman y Paz Vega.
– ¿De qué trata el argumento?
– Cuenta la historia de una cajera (Paz Vega) que trabaja en un supermercado en un barrio pobre de Los Ángeles. Una noche llega al supermercado Morgan Freeman, actor de cine también en la película, que quiere informarse sobre el personaje que va a desempeñar en su próximo trabajo. La película cuenta la historia de su relación y cómo se ayudan mutuamente ...

2
– A mí me gustan todas las comedias románticas como *Tú la letra yo la música* porque son sencillas.
– ¿Quién dirigió esa película?
– El director es Marc Lawrence si recuerdo bien.
– Y los actores, ¿quiénes son?
– Pues, los protagonistas son Hugh Grant y Drew Barrymore.
– ¿De qué trata?
– Pues, trata de Alex Fletcher (Hugh Grant), una estrella de pop en horas bajas. Conoce a una chica (Drew Barrymore) que le ayuda a escribir la letra de una canción y así termina recuperando su autoestima.

3
- Prefiero los thrillers psicológicos y las aventuras de intriga como *El último Bourne*.
- ¿Qué es eso?
- Pues es la tercera película de Doug Liman y Paul Greengrass, basada en la novela de Robert Ludlum en la que Matt Damon desempeña el papel de Jason Bourne, un agente secreto que tiene amnesia. Bourne sigue buscando su identidad por todo el planeta, incluso en Madrid, donde rodaron varias escenas.

2e Students discuss in pairs or as a whole class exercise which films they consider to have been the biggest box office hits during the year. They then rate them using the grid.

P 45, Se pronuncia así

Accents and stress
Take students through the advice step by step and ensure they understand.

hablo	mesa	independiente
hablas	hablan	mesas independientes
hablar	actitud	corral
jardín	último	jóvenes

A They then read the words and decide which ones need a written accent.

Answers:
película; fantasía; romántico

To reinforce the different genres of film students could play a guessing game. One person thinks of a film and the rest of the class ask questions to find out the title.

- ¿Es una comedia?
  (No).
- ¿Es una fantasía?
  (Sí).
- ¿Se trata de?
  OR
- ¿Quién es el director?

Protagonistas del mundo del cine

Grammar focus
- *lo* and *lo que*

Skills focus
- Speaking – putting forward ideas and opinions

Key language
- *lo bueno / lo malo; lo mejor / lo peor; lo que más me gusta / me interesa /*
- *protagonista, guionista, desempeñar un papel, estrenar, rodar una película, impactante, chocante, tratar de, destacar, el enfoque, no se puede negar que, por un lado ... por el otro*

Resources
- Students' Book pages 46 and 47
- CD 1, track 34
- Hojas 11, 12

1a Remind students about the work covered on reading strategies in Unit 2. Students then read the text about Gael García Bernal and his first film as a director – *Déficit*.

Students look in the text for equivalent phrases at first without resorting to a dictionary, and then using a dictionary if need be.

Answers:
1 *compañía productora*
2 *no sólo ... sino que también*
3 *desempeñar el papel de*
4 *el guión*
5 *se trata de*
6 *a pesar de que*
7 *lo que sea que hagas*
8 *rodar*

1b Students choose the most suitable answer from the multiple choice given.

Answers: 1 *c*   2 *c*   3 *a*   4 *a*   5 *c*   6 *b*

2a Students listen to the recording about women in Spanish cinema to get an overall idea of the context. They then study the questions to give them a clearer focus. They can listen a second time if they are unsure of the answers and then indicate which are the three correct ones.

Answers:
2, 5, 7

2b Students explain why they think the others are incorrect.

 2c Students listen again and make notes in order to write a brief resumé in English under the given headings.

There are several Spanish film stars mentioned in this recording, so to follow up, students could research them and present their details at a later time.

P 46, actividad 2a

Hoy celebramos a la mujer española como actriz de cine y destacamos a la actriz madrileña Penélope Cruz.
Su vida comenzó el 28 de abril de 1974. Según ella y toda su familia, Penélope siempre fue una

---

niña enérgica y voluntariosa que pasaba mucho tiempo en casa de su abuela.

Debutó con la película *Belle Epoque* de Fernando Trueba en 1993 y después siguieron otras muchas como *Carne Trémula* de Pedro Almodóvar y la película española *Abre los Ojos*, que ganó varios Goyas – premio español equivalente a los Oscars. De allí se fue a Hollywood donde desempeñó el mismo papel en la versión estadounidense de la película, *Vanilla Sky*, con Tom Cruise.

La fama no la ha cambiado y se sigue comportando igual con sus hermanos Eduardo y Mónica, que son dos gotas de agua. Mónica sigue los pasos de su hermana mayor; después de ser una de los protagonistas de la serie *Un paso adelante*, que tuvo mucho éxito en España, ha participado en varias películas. Penélope forma parte de un impresionante grupo de actrices españolas – Ana Belén, Carmen Maura, Victoria Abril y Ana Torrent. Ana trabajó con Saura en *Cría Cuervos* y Victoria Abril protagonizó con Javier Bardem *Tu Nombre Envenena Mis Sueños* entre otras muchas.

Su estreno en inglés fue la película *The Hi Lo Country* de Stephen Frears, quien la considera como Venus. Penélope se sintió tan orgullosa de su papel en dicha película que donó todo su salario a un fondo de caridad de la Madre Teresa.

Decididamente ha tenido papeles muy diversos: una monja embarazada con Sida, una novelista, una cocinera brasileña y la amante del ministro nazi Joseph Goebbels. Su película *Fan Fan La Tulipe* triunfó en el Festival de Cine de Cannes.

3a Students read the text on Juan Carlos Rulfo and decide if the sentences that follow are true or false.

Answers:
1 ✗   2 ✓   3 ✓   4 ✗   5 ✗

3b Students work out the meaning of the title ('chip off the old block' / 'like father, like son').

3c Students find synonyms for the words and phrases listed.

Answers:
más importantes; dotes; becas; rodar; seleccionada; trascender; convertirse en; de la actualidad

Técnica

Putting forward opinions.
Remind students about the work covered in Unit 1 pages 20–22 about agreeing and disagreeing. They now add more phrases to their list and consider the different ways of expressing themselves.

A Students match the phrases to one of the three sample ways.

Answers:
1 *Por un lado ... por el otro; No solamente ... sino también ...*
2 *Hay que considerar que; No se puede negar que ... Se podría creer que ...; Se supone que ...*
3 *Creo que ...; No podemos olivdarnos de que ...; A mi modo de ver ...*

Remind students about making value judgements and therefore needing to use the subjunctive in the subordinate clause.

B Students discuss more fully than previously the merits and faults of a film. Encourage them to use more technical vocabulary connected to cinema. Show them a commentary in English to help them appreciate what is required of them if they want to raise their language to a more sophisticated level.

4 For a bit of fun students rate the ten Hollywood actors they think are the most important. This could be played as an elimination game until they have five main actors.

5 To sum up this section, students write a critical synopsis of a film using as much of the language covered so far as they can.

El Teatro

Grammar focus
♦ Imperfect tense and *iba a* + infinitive

Skills focus
♦ Discussion tactics and giving opinions continued

Key language
el teatro, dramaturgo, títeres, máscaras, espectáculo, la cárcel, reintegrar, la condena, el delito, los presos

Resources
♦ Students' Book pages 48 and 49
♦ CD 1, track 35
♦ Hojas 13, 14
♦ Grammar Workbook page 41

1a Students read the text giving a brief synopsis of two contrasting forms of theatre in Spain. They look for synonyms for the phrases given.

Answers:
destaca; mundialmente conocidas; empezó a hacerse conocido; entre otros; un grupo itinerante; que tanto prometía; años más tarde; títeres gigantescos sobre zancos; que se verían representados

1b Ask students to answer the two questions in their own words as far as possible.

1c Students then look for word families following the example. They could offer further examples of their own. Explain that this can also be a useful strategy in reading.

1 *dramaturgo – drama – dramático*
2 *poesía – poeta – poema*
3 *pintor – pintar – la pintura – pintoresco*
4 *músico – la música – musical*
5 *títeres – tiritero*
6 *compositor – composición – componer*

2a Students read the text on prison theatre and decide if the ideas listed below are supported in the text. Get them to use their own words to answer.

Answers should include words and phrases from the text to back up why students have reached this conclusion.

2b Students listen to the discussion and list the positive and negative opinions offered. They could list them first under 'Jorge' and 'Isabel', and then decide if they are positive or negative. Jorge presents a negative attitude and Isabel a more positive one.

P 49, actividad 2b

– Isabel, ¿te has fijado en lo que han escrito hoy en el periódico sobre las cárceles?
– No, Jorge. ¿Qué dicen?
– Parece que ahora las cárceles son hoteles de lujo y hasta permiten espectáculos de teatro.
– ¿Cómo? ¿Qué quieres decir con eso?
– Bueno pues, es obvio que hoy no se toma en serio ni el castigo ni la condena, sólo hay libertad para todo y todos.
– Pero si los prisioneros están encarcelados no tienen libertad para nada. Tienen que mantenerse ocupados con algo y es mejor que hagan algo útil.
– ¿Te parece útil una representación teatral?
– Claro que sí, porque no solamente les permite expresarse sino también les ayuda a comprenderse a sí mismos por medio del drama – me parece buena idea.
– Nada de eso; somos demasiado comprensivos con ellos; no vale la pena ocuparse de ellos. La mayoría son mala gente y sería mejor encerrarlos y perder la llave.
– ¡Vaya! ¡Qué opiniones tan horribles! La única manera de reintegrar a la gente en la sociedad es dándole la oportunidad de hacer algo que valga la pena y dejándole recuperar su autoestima.
– ¡Bahhhh! ¡Qué ideas tan estúpidas y sosas las tuyas!

2c In pairs, students now discuss what they have heard and give their own opinion. Encourage them to re-use all the phrases and words learnt so far for expressing opinions and discussing ideas.

Gramática

Imperfect tense.
Take students through the examples to ensure they appreciate the subtleties and nuances of language. Students will meet time clauses such as *acabar de* later.

A Students read the two texts again and select the verbs in the imperfect tense. They should be able to explain why they think this tense is used.

3 Students then use the imperfect tense to describe a scene of a play or film, using the questions as prompts.

De música y músicos

Grammar focus
♦ Object pronouns – direct and indirect

Skills focus
♦ Speaking from notes
♦ Structuring a presentation

Key language
♦ *le, lo, la; los, las; se lo*
♦ *homenaje / homenajeado; cantautora; digan lo que digan; sea como sea; pase lo que pase; a mi modo de ver; a mi parecer; sin lugar a dudas; es cierto que; hay que reconocer que; estrepitoso*

Resources
♦ Students' Book pages 50 and 51
♦ CD 1, tracks 36–37
♦ Hoja 15
♦ Grammar Workbook page 23

1a Students listen to the programme and decide which of the questions are correct. They correct the incorrect ones. They should look through the *frases clave* to make sure they know what these mean.

Answers:
1 X *Menciona Juanes, Shakira, Carlos Vives.*
   Y *una cubana Celia Cruz.*
2 X *Menciona cinco clases de premios.*
3 ✓ 4 ✓ 5 X *Era actor.*

P 50, actividad 1

– Sin lugar a dudas, Colombia está en la cima de la música latina y más aún tras el triunfo del colombiano Juanes, que consiguió cinco Grammy Latinos en una gala de homenaje a Celia Cruz, la "reina de la salsa cubana".

> El cantautor triunfó al llevarse los premios para Grabación del Año, Álbum del Año, Canción del Año, Mejor Solista Vocal y Mejor Canción de Rock.
> Pero vamos a ver lo que opinan nuestros reporteros juveniles.
> – Juanes me flipa y me encanta su nombre verdadero, Juan Esteban Aristizábal – tiene una sonoridad tan profunda – igual que sus canciones.
> – Digan lo que digan, Shakira es para mí la mejor de todas las cantautoras – ella también ganó mogollón de premios incluidos varios Grammy y prefiero su estilo rock – además es una guitarrista fenomenal. Y la letra de sus canciones es genial.
> – ¿Y qué decís de Carlos Vives – gran actor como era y cantante estupendo como es ahora que interpreta vallenatos antiguos, modernos – un poco de todo? Sea como sea haré todo lo posible para ir a su próximo concierto.

2a Students listen to another programme and make notes using the questions as prompts.

Answers:

1   *baladas lentas, flamenco pop, rock pop*
2   *la salsa, grunge, garage*
3   *los latinos no deben cantar en inglés sino en español*
4   *es lo mejor del momento*

> p 50, actividad 2
>
> Buenas tardes, amigos poperos. ¿Qué opinamos de la música favorita del momento? A ver. Sin lugar a dudas las opiniones varían como siempre, pero los votos van para la música lenta de las baladas y de los boleros porque se entiende mejor la letra y son super bailables cuando uno sale de noche.
> Una crítica negativa es que los artistas latinos siempre terminan cantando en inglés en vez de conformarse con su lengua materna y mi opinión es que deberían promocionar el español y no el gringo.
> Además es cierto que la salsa ha pasado un poco de moda al igual que la música grunge y garage, pero hay que reconocer que el flamenco pop ha ganado popularidad.
> De hecho, a mi parecer la fusión del rockpop con un toque de instrumentos regionales es lo mejor del momento. A ver lo que opináis, queridos radioaficionados. Llamad o envíad un mensaje al número de siempre …

2b Students use the words given and the *frases clave* to write about the current musical scene in the UK as they see it.

3 Students choose an appropriate word to describe the various musical styles.

Gramática

Object pronouns – direct and indirect.
If students are secure in using pronouns then they could read through the grammar box on their own. Otherwise, take them through each stage carefully. Pronouns are often overlooked in language but they play a key part in understanding longer sentences. As students progress in their ability to write more sophisticated language they will need to use pronouns more and more, so they need to have a secure grasp of them.

A Students write sentences using the verbs given.

Answers:

1   *Siempre veo las emisiones de EastEnders.*
    Yo no, las grabo en un vídeo.
2   *Siempre escucho la radio por la tarde.*
    Yo no, la escucho por la noche.
3   *Siempre hago mis deberes en seguida.*
    Yo no, los hago el día siguiente.
4   *Siempre me baño por la noche.*
    Yo no, me ducho por la mañana.

4a and 4b Students follow the example and complete the dialogues.

Answers:

3a *Se los regaló su padre; Nos las regaló su hermana; Se la regalaron mis padres*
3b *Iba a dársela yo / Ya se la he dado;*
    Iba a dárselos yo / Ya se los he dado;
    Iba a dárselos yo / Ya se los he dado.

4a Students read the text on Juan Diego Flórez and Luis Miguel and complete the sentences in their own words.

Possible answers to include:

1   *dos cantantes jóvenes – estilos diferentes*
2   *Elvis – la música criolla*
3   *a los 23 años*
4   *La Scala – Kew Gardens*
5   *pop o baladas latinas*
6   *vendido más de 52 millones de discos*
7   *pera llenar el Madison Square Garden*

5b Students choose two contrasting singers and give a brief comparative analysis.

Técnica

Speaking from notes and structuring a presentation. Students read through the advice.

La expresión musical

Grammar focus
- Compound tenses using *haber* – the pluperfect tense

Skills focus
- How to approach speaking stimulus material

Key language
ciego; componer; compositor; composiciones; pasar hambre; la penuria; folklórico; flamencas; lo clásico; lo baroco; hacer impacto; heredar; lanzar una carrera; se está haciendo famoso; lograr hacer una cosa

Resources
- Students' Book pages 52 and 53
- CD 1, track 38
- Grammar Workbook page 45

1a Students read the obituary of Joaquín Rodrigo. They use this as a basis for an oral presentation. They should use their own words as far as possible. They may need a reminder about how to prepare a presentation – so refer them back to page 51.

1b Students research the musicians listed, or any other Spanish or Latin American musicians of their choice, and prepare an oral presentation, making sure to include the points required.

Gramática

The pluperfect tense.
Students read through the information. Ask them questions about it to elicit whether they have fully understood.

A Students look for examples of the pluperfect tense in the text.

B Students write the sentences in Spanish.

Answers:
1 *Antes de llegar a ser cantante de ópera Juan Diego Flórez había querido centor música de pop como los Beatles.*
2 *Luis Miguel había hecho una gira por Latinoamérica cuando dio este concierto en Málaga.*
3 *No había escuchado de él antes de que apareciera en Nueva York.*

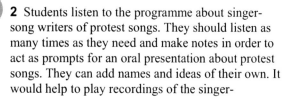

2 Students listen to the programme about singer-song writers of protest songs. They should listen as many times as they need and make notes in order to act as prompts for an oral presentation about protest songs. They can add names and ideas of their own. It would help to play recordings of the singer-

songwriters, and use some of their verses as reading texts.

> **P 52, actividad 2**
>
> La canción de protesta tiene una larga historia tanto en España como en Latinoamérica. En los años 60 del siglo pasado cantantes como Joan Manuel Serrat y Joan Baez ya levantaron sus voces.
> Al mismo tiempo en Latinoamérica la voz de Soledad Bravo, nacida en España pero educada en Venezuela, empezaba a hacer impacto. Heredó sus convicciones políticas de su padre y en su primer álbum incluyó la canción de Carlos Puebla "Hasta Siempre", un tributo a Che Guevara, que hace poco resurgió como número uno en Francia.
> Igualmente las palabras del guatemalteco Ricardo Arjona hablan de la pobreza, el dolor y la desesperación de la gente de su país. Su canción "Jesús Verbo No Sustantivo", que escribió en Buenos Aires, Argentina, lanzó su carrera con Sony. Otra canción "Mojado" de su último álbum "Adentro" habla del sufrimiento de los inmigrantes ilegales en los Estados Unidos.
> Por último actualmente es muy famoso el colombiano Juanes, Juan Esteban, con canciones que posan preguntas sobre los temas universales del terrorismo y la violencia, que ha sufrido en su ciudad natal de Medellín.
> Los tres logran combinar una mezcla interesante de liricismo y folklore además de ritmos populares como salsa y rock y es por eso que tienen un atractivo universal.

Técnica
How to approach speaking stimulus material.

Ask students to read through the advice and discuss the ideas before they complete activity 3.

The activity offers information in English and students need to be able to act as interpreters and help a Spanish-speaking person to understand not only the content of the leaflet, but also to answer questions based on it.

Gramática en acción

Grammar focus
- *lo* and *lo que*

Resources
- Students' Book page 54

Read through this section with students asking them for further examples of their own to make sure they have fully understood how lo and lo que function in Spanish.

A Students read the text again and find the relevant phrases.

Answers:

lo interesante; lo mejor; lo que nos interesa; lo que sea que hogas; lo político; lo más importante; lo que comenta Bernal

♦ *Iba a ...*
Students read the reminder section about how to say what they are, or were going to do.

B Now students take turns as A or B and practise orally saying what they are, or were going to do.

♦ Past tenses
Students read the reminder section about mixed past tenses. First they practise recognising them from reading texts. Add a listening text as well so that they practise listening out for mixed tenses.

C Then they read the texts on pages 48 and 52 again and make a list of the verbs used and indicate their tense. This can be done orally or as a written exercise.

♦ Sequencing tenses
Students read the section about the need to be precise in identifying which tense is required when writing. They then complete tasks D, E and F using a mixture of past tenses both orally and in writing.

♦ Pronouns
Students read the reminder about the order of pronouns and copy out the table in the grammar section (task G).

A escoger

Resources
♦ Students' Book page 55
♦ CD 1, tracks 39–40

1a Students read the text on flamenco and then decide if the statements which follow are made in the text.

Answers:
1 ✓   2 ✓   3 ✓   4 ✕   5 ✕

1b Students find evidence from the text to back up their decisions.

2 Students research and then prepare an oral presentation about flamenco. They could illustrate this with music if practical.

Se pronuncia así

Intonation.
Students read the information and then put it into practice.

A They copy out the examples, marking the *sinalefa* and *entrelazamiento*.

B They listen to the poem and practise the pronounciation.

P 55, Se pronuncia así

Toco la guitarra.
¿Qué instrumento tocas?
¿Tienes una flauta?
Tú tienes una flauta y yo tengo una guitarra.

Voy a ir a la alcaldía.
Los otros niños están en el hotel.

P 55, Se pronuncia así actividad B

Soy gaucho y entiéndaló
Como mi lengua los esplica;
Para mí la tierra es chica
Y pudiera ser mayor.
Ni la víbora me pica
Ni quema mi frente el sol.

Nací como nace el peje,
En el fondo de la mar;
Naides me puede quitar
Aquello que Dios me dio;
Lo que al mundo truje yo
Del mundo lo he de llevar.

Mi gloria es vivir tan libre
Como el pájaro del cielo;
No hago nido en el suelo,
Ande hay tanto que sufrir;
Y naides me ha de seguir
Cuando yo remuento el vuelo.

Unidad 4 Construyendo el futuro

Unit objectives

By the end of this unit students will be able to:

♦ Discuss the contribution of young people to society
♦ Compare popular activities and concerns of young people in Spanish-speaking countries and their own country
♦ Consider and offer arguments against the negative stereotyping of young people
♦ Analyse young people's interest in celebrity

Grammar

By the end of this unit students will be able to:

♦ Use the subjunctive mood in past tenses: imperfect, perfect and pluperfect
♦ Use the personal *a* when necessary

Skills

By the end of this unit students will be able to:

♦ Structure paragraphs and longer pieces of writing
♦ Write sentences including relative pronouns
♦ Use Spanish time expressions, recognising where tense usage is different from English
♦ Tackle gap-fill sentences

Resources

♦ Students' Book pages 56–57

1 Ask students to think about personality adjectives that they already know, particularly those that describe positively young people. A list of adjectives in English is provided so that they have a starting point that will give them numerous possibilities for each of the letters outstanding in the acrostic, with many cognates to get them started. Students should be encouraged to think of additional adjectives.

Answers:

brave – *valiente*; charming – *encantador*;
daring – *atrevido*; enthusiastic – *entusiasta*;
happy – *joviales*; hard-working – *trabajadores*;
normal – *normales*; original – *originales*
outstanding – *sobresalientes*;
passionate – *apasionados*; seductive – *seductores*;
tenacious – *tenaces*; versatile – *versátiles*;
vibrant – *vivaces*; well-mannered – *educados*;
wise – *sabios*

2 Now students complete the personality test and check their results. The activity can be used to open a speaking debate about tolerance in society and among the young, as well as subjects such as discrimination.

3a Students read statements and work out what the survey questions would have been.

3b Students reflect the statements in 3a and discuss differences between young people´s habits in the twocountries. Perhaps statements 3 and 6 present the best discussion points because probably only a small minority of 15 to 25 year-olds return home after 6 a.m. in most parts of the UK, while the percentages of young people owning games consoles and computers is likely to be much higher.

4 Students order the leisure activities listed from most popular to least popular, according to what they think is more common in Spain and then they compare their answers with the answers given. You should explain that the phenomenon of *El botellón* is not accepted in Spanish law, but the Spanish police and law enforcement agencies are struggling to keep it under control.

Los jóvenes: ¿Demonios o angelitos?

Grammar focus

♦ The subjunctive mood in past tenses

Resources

♦ Students' Book pages 58–59
♦ CD 2, track 2
♦ Hoja 16
♦ Grammar Workbook page 54

1a Students read for gist and decide in which paragraph each idea is mentioned.

Answers:
a *3;* **b** *4;* **c** *1;* **d** *2*

1b Students apply more detailed reading to decide which of the accusations are made about young people.

Answers:

perezosos, ingratos, egoístas, degenerados, desobedientes

1c Students decide how each accusation is justified in the text.

Answers:
Perezosos: no estudian ni trabajan.
Egoístas: quieren tener todo / no contribuyen a la sociedad.
Degenerados: pasan de todo / se dedican al sexo, a las drogas y a la violencia / no conocen la responsabilidad.
Desobedientes: no hacen caso a nadie.
Ingratos: no hacen caso a sus padres a quienes deben todo / quieren todo pero no contribuyen a la sociedad.

2a Students listen to the recording for gist and decide whether the speakers agree with Delia's opinion of today's youth.

P 58, actividad 2a

Nuria Yo creo que Delia tiene una visión demasiado negativa de los jóvenes de hoy. Por supuesto que hay algunos jóvenes que viven de los padres, pero eso se debe a la falta de oportunidades y al precio inasequible de la vivienda y el coste de la vida en general. Hay muchísimos jóvenes que se interesan por lo que pasa a su alrededor, aunque algunos son un poco inmaduros. Pero a mí me parece que a Delia se le ha olvidado que ella también fue joven. El abismo generacional siempre ha existido y la resistencia al cambio es normal.

Miguel Creo que Delia no conoce a muchos jóvenes: quizás haya tenido una mala experiencia con los que conoce y por eso generaliza en sus acusaciones. Hay muchos jóvenes emprendedores que buscan salir adelante a base de esfuerzo y trabajo. Algunos son muy creativos, y eso sumado a su esfuerzo hace que lleven adelante proyectos de nuevos negocios, formen empresas y den trabajo a otros jóvenes. Pero sobre todo, yo creo que los jóvenes de hoy tenemos más esperanzas y ganas de vivir en un mundo mejor.

Marta Hace falta tener en cuenta que hay muchos jóvenes que para nada se pueden identificar con la opinión de la juventud de esa carta. ¿Qué me dices de todos los jóvenes atletas que trabajan para superarse? Empiezan desde muy niños y trabajan muy duro. También están los que se preocupan por la ecología y actúan diariamente para contrarrestar el impacto del hombre en el medio ambiente: estos trabajan para crear un mundo mejor para las generaciones futuras. ¿No es una contribución a la comunidad? Y también están los jóvenes que desempeñan labores altruistas. Por ejemplo, yo he sido voluntario en instituciones para niños desamparados y discapacitados desde que tenía 14 años, junto con otros chicos igual de jóvenes. Me enfada el veredicto de Delia, creo que nos juzga a todos por igual y los estereotipos siempre son injustos.

Antonio Creo que Delia debería aceptar que la sociedad cambia y que los cambios no son siempre negativos. Reconozco que la juventud de hoy tiene mala fama pero desde que el mundo es mundo, los

jóvenes han intentado romper con lo conocido y salirse con la suya. Seguro que ella no es ni la mitad de tolerante que los jóvenes de hoy. Nuestra mentalidad es mucho más amplia, y tenemos una mente más abierta, capaz de aceptar nuevas posturas y nuevas ideas. Antes, era muy raro que un joven estuviera a favor del aborto o la homosexualidad porque los padres les hacían creer que eso era malo. Afortunadamente ahora hay jóvenes de mente más abierta. Además, tenemos una mente más desarrollada y somos capaces de adquirir nuevos conocimientos más rápidamente. Por ejemplo en el caso del uso de las computadoras y otras tecnologías.

Answer:
Los jóvenes no están de acuerdo con Delia.

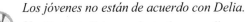

2b Students listen again to the recording and make notes of the positive values of youth as they are mentioned.

Gramática

Revise the main uses of the subjunctive in wanting, requesting and advising sentences, in sentences expressing value judgements, doubt or improbability and in *cuando* clauses. Work through the grammar box in the Students' Book.

Answers:
A
pudiera, pudieras, pudiera, pudiéramos, pudierais, pudieran
OR
pudiese, pudieses, pudiese, pudiésemos, pudieseis, pudiesen
hiciera, hicieras, hiciera, hiciéramos, hicierais, hicieran
OR
hiciese, hicieses, hiciese, hiciésemos, hicieseis, hiciesen
viviera, vivieras, viviera, viviéramos, vivierais, vivieran
OR
viviese, vivieses, viviese, viviésemos, vivieseis, viviesen
tuviera, tuvieras, tuviera, tuviéramos, tuvierais, tuvieran
OR
tuviese, tuvieses, tuviese, tuviésemos, tuvieseis, tuviesen
fuera, fueras, fuera, fuéramos, fuerais, fueran
OR
fuese, fueses, fuese, fuésemos, fueseis, fuesen

B

1 *saliera* or *saliese*

2 *compraran* or *comprasen*

3 *suspendieran* or *suspendiesen*

4 *condujera* or *condujese*

5 *pusieras* or *pusieses*

3 Students reflect on the strengths and weaknesses of the young people of today and yesterday and they present their views to the rest of the class for open discussion.

4 Students write a letter in defence of young people using the ideas given on these two pages. Remind students to attempt the use of the imperfect subjunctive by revising the grammar box and its examples.

Como abejas atrapadas en la miel

Grammar focus

♦ Relative pronouns

Skills focus

♦ Writing paragraphs

Key language

Me parece que ...
Me sorprende que ...
Me alegra que ...
Me desagrada que ... + subjuntivo
Me da asco que ...
Es escandaloso que ...
Es una lástima que ...

Resources

♦ Students' Book pages 60–61

♦ CD 2, track 3

♦ Grammar Workbook page 26

1a Students read the paragraph about the changing face of fame and express their opinion using the vocabulary provided.

1b Students write a list of the famous people who receive the most media coverage in their country currently, and compare their list with that of a partner.

1c In pairs, students go through their list answering questions 1–4.

2a Students discuss their opinions about the desire of young people to imitate famous people.

2b Students listen to the speakers and decide who mentions each of the statements 1–6.

	P 60, actividad 2b
Marga	Porque tratan de parecerse a ellos, porque saben que la forma en que tal o cual famoso actúa y es, está aceptada o asimilada por la sociedad. Así el camino es más corto y más fácil.
Maria José	No todos los famosos dan mal ejemplo, algunos comparten lo que tienen y su éxito no se les sube a la cabeza sino que lo utilizan para causas altruistas y ayudas sociales tanto a nivel económico como a nivel propagandístico ya que tienen el poder de hacer llegar su causa a las masas.
Alicia	Lo hacen para ser aceptados ... para ser un tanto populares ... es como esas mujeres que quieren ser como las que salen en las telenovelas. Son muy superficiales, y además no tienen una personalidad propia ni original ya que sólo imitan lo que ven en las telenovelas.
Nacho	En realidad creo que es por falta de amor propio, de no saber valorar lo que tienen, y no darse cuenta de que, al fin de cuentas, serán más felices sabiendo por qué son valiosos y no imitando a gente famosa. Creo que la necesidad de aceptación y de reconocimiento es ahora muy fuerte en la sociedad, y buscan una manera sencilla de ser aceptados.
Iván	¿La verdad? Simple, por falta de talento propio.
Iñaki	La verdad ... pues no sé, yo no hago eso, si lo hiciera tal vez te respondería pero no sé. Somos muchos los jóvenes con opiniones propias y que no nos dejamos influenciar tan fácilmente. ¡No es oro todo lo que reluce!

Answers:

1 *Nacho* 2 *Nacho* 3 *María José* 4 *Alicia*
5 *Alicia* 6 *María José*

Técnica

Paragraphs.

Answers:

A

Introduction:
Parece que cada día ... llegaban a la fama.

Presentation of the situation:
En mi infancia ... o mejor dicho 'famosillo'.

Explanation / information and argument:
a través ... dudoso talento y porvenir.

Evidence to support argument:
He aquí los culpables ... no recuerdo.

B The answers below are for guidance as some of the phrases may fit in more than one category depending on the context.

Answers:

1 – Continuing or adding an idea: *quizás la verdad es más compleja / al mismo tiempo / más importante aun es / además*

2 – Qualifying an idea: *el mejor ejemplo sería / ...*

3 – Contrasting or denying: *a pesar de / claro ..., pero ...*

Gramática

Relative pronouns. Refer students to the relevant grammar section of the Students' Book and the Grammar Workbook.

Answers:

A

1 – *Buenafuente, quien ha escrito nueve libros, es un presentador de televisión muy popular.*

2 – *El nuevo Gran hermano, que empieza hoy, parece muy extravagante.*

3 – *La cantante Chenoa, cuya nacionalidad es argentina, lanzó su primer álbum en 2002 después de su éxito en OT.*

4 – *La fama de David Bustamante, la cual (or que) se debe a su paso por OT1, ha resultado en una carrera musical de mucho éxito.*

3a Students read the article about David Bisbal and order the paragraphs so that it presents a coherent piece in a logical order. Remind students to revise the Técnica section on page 60.

Answer:

3, 1, 2, 4

3b Students read the passage about David Bisbal, and try to think of a brief title for each paragraph.

Answers:

Some suggested titles:

1 *trayectoria discográfica / discografía / éxito discográfico*

2 *¿Quién es? / un joven con talento / presentación*

3 *sus inicios / ¿De dónde proviene? / el comienzo*

4 *un joven con principios / conciencia humana / su contribución a la sociedad*

3c Students read the text thoroughly from a grammatical perspective. They identify the relative pronouns within it and what they substitute in each case.

1   ... *que fue su debut discográfico ... (su primer álbum)*

     ... *cuya fama le precede... (Bisbal)*

2   ... *que emergen de los reality ... (algunos famosos)*

     ... *que se les otorga ...(la fama)*

3   ... *que fue uno de los primeros ... (Operación Triunfo)*

     ... *el cual elegiría ... (el público)*

4   ... *cuya meta es denunciar ... (un conmovedor tema)*

     ...*que esto supone para los ... (el uso de niños en conflictos armados)*

4 Students pick a famous person and write a similar article making sure to use the correct relative pronouns to link their sentences and avoid repetition. Remind students to revise the Gramática and Técnica sections and encourage them to research someone linked to a Spanish-speaking country.

Juventud de contrastes

Grammar focus

♦ The personal *a*, time clauses

Resources

♦ Students' Book pages 62–63
♦ CD 2, tracks 4–5
♦ Hoja 17
♦ Grammar Workbook pages 20, 38

1a Students read the two contrasting articles for gist and discuss similar problems and traditions in their own country.

1b Students answer questions 1–3 according to their own opinion.

1c Students discuss in pairs the advantages and disadvantages of belonging to a group of *Castellers*. They must reflect on the implications that this has on family, health, social life and community.

Encourage students to do some internet research on *els castellers* so that they can gauge the present extent of this tradition and the impressive variety of human towers that the different groups build. You should explain that 30 August is the feast day of St Felix and it is the most important day of the year for celebrating the tradition of *els castellers*. Several of the most successful groups compete against each other to build the best / tallest / most intricate towers. New members are accepted into the groups from age 4, which is the earliest age in which the child is allowed to climb up the towers. Each layer of the towers has progressively younger participants; those that crown them on the top two layers are generally under 7 years of age. Despite the fact it might look like a dangerous tradition, and last year the law enforced the use of helmets for the two children at the top, in fact, the annual total of fatal and serious accidents resulting from skiing are far more significant.

Check out www.castellersdevilafranca.cat for some impressive photos and video footage of one the most famous of the Catalan *Colla* of *Castellers*.

2 Students listen to the recording and answer the questions.

Answers:

1 *Organización Cultural de Reyes y Reinas Latinos de Cataluña*

2 *En Cataluña*

3 *Recibir ayudas y subvenciones de la administración / incentivos para la integración de los jóvenes latinoamericanos*

4 *Terminar con prejuicios / percepción negativa de la banda*

5 *Educación de los jóvenes inmigrantes / promoción de las relaciones interculturales*

6 *Talleres de formación / competiciones deportivas / creación de un documental / un CD*

P 62, actividad 2

– Hoy nace la OCRRLC, la Organización Cultural de Reyes y Reinas Latinos de Cataluña. La OCRRLC es descendiente de la banda juvenil los Latin Kings que finalmente y después de largas negociaciones, ha conseguido ser reconocida como una asociación legal en la Comunidad Autónoma de Cataluña. Ser legales permitirá a sus organizadores recibir ayudas y subvenciones de la administración, así como incentivos para su causa: la integración en Cataluña de los jóvenes latinoamericanos inmigrantes, para que estos tengan igualdad de oportunidades.

Con este cambio quieren terminar con los prejuicios y la percepción negativa asociada con la banda Latin Kings, y entre sus objetivos se encuentran la educación de los jóvenes inmigrantes y la promoción de las relaciones interculturales.

Escuchemos a la presidenta de la organización:

– Algunas actividades ya están planeadas para los próximos meses o ya se están llevando a cabo, por ejemplo los talleres de formación para ayudar a los socios a ser más competitivos en el terreno laboral. También se están organizando competiciones deportivas que esperan sacar a los nuestros de la calle. Además, estamos organizando ayudas para los indigentes y la creación de un documental sobre nuestra propia entidad para ayudar a la gente a entendernos, e incluso estamos planeando un CD, pues la música es un método de comunicación muy arraigado entre los jóvenes.

– La Organización Cultural de Reyes y Reinas Latinos de Cataluña es un movimiento muy positivo y se espera que otras Comunidades Autónomas puedan seguir el ejemplo del gobierno catalán. Asimismo, quizás el éxito de esta asociación anime a los Ñetas, los

---

– tradicionales adversarios de los Latin Kings, a seguir su ejemplo.

Answers:

1 – *convertirse* 2 – *es* 3 – *ayudar; encontrar; planean* 4 – *intenta; promover* 5 – *espera; sigan* 6 – *son*

Gramática

The personal *a*. Refer students to the relevant grammar section of the Students' Book and the Grammar Workbook.

Answers:

A

1 *permitirá a sus organizadores*

2 *escuchemos a la presidenta*

3 *ayudar a los socios*

4 *sacar a los nuestros*

5 *ayudar a la gente*

6 *anime a los Ñetas*

B

Vi a la víctima siendo golpeada por un miembro banda.

Vi el accidente cuando pasó.

Escuché el ruido de la pelea.

Escuché a los chicos gritar.

Presenté mi proyecto de integración cultural.

Presenté a mi novio a mi abuela.

3a Students read the letter and discuss what is, in their opinion, the best age to have children.

3b Students reflect about the things that one ought to consider before having children and make a list.

3c Students listen to Alicia, Sara and Elena and decide who gives Elisa each piece of advice.

P 63, actividad 3c

Alicia Puede ser que sientas que falta algo en tu vida y por eso crees que el amor de un hijo va a llenar ese espacio. Si quieres que tus hijos te respeten y te admiren, consigue un buen trabajo y un buen hombre antes de tenerlos y el resto es coser y cantar; bueno, casi. Creo que sería un error tener un bebé en estos momentos porque tú misma admites que no quieres estar atada.

Sara Quizás deberías buscar trabajo de niñera o algo parecido. Así tendrías la oportunidad de cuidar a bebés y niños y tener una experiencia realista. Sé que no es lo mismo que tener tus propios hijos pero te daría una idea de cómo va a ser.

> **Elena** Sabes que puede ser un problema así que yo te recomiendo que busques otro método anticonceptivo en el que no tengas que pensar cuando estés con tu novio. Estudia, consigue un buen trabajo y entonces piénsalo otra vez.

Answers:

1 *Elena*   2 *Alicia*   3 *Sara*   4 *Elena*
5 *Alicia*   6 *Alicia*

3d Students write their own answer to Elisa's letter.

Gramática

Time clauses. Refer students to the relevant grammar section of the Students' Book and the Grammar Workbook.

Answers:

A

1 *Hace tres años que pertenezco al equipo.*
2 *Acabo de subscribirme a un nuevo gimnasio.*
3 *Hacía un año que el club estaba cerrado cuando abrió de nuevo.*

Jóvenes adultos

Grammar focus

♦ The perfect and pluperfect subjunctives

Skills focus

♦ Filling gaps

Resources

♦ Students' Book pages 64–65
♦ CD 2, tracks 6–7
♦ Hojas 18, 19, 20
♦ Grammar Workbook page 54

1a Students think about what they are allowed to do at what age and try to guess if the same applies in Spain.

 1b Students listen to check their answers.

> P 64, actividad 1b
>
> – ¿A qué edad puedes entrar en un bar en España?
> – Pues, si es un restaurante o un bar de tapas o algo así es muy común que los jóvenes vayan con sus padres, pero para beber alcohol y para entrar en ciertos bares – bares de copas – para beber, tienes que tener 18 años.
> – ¿Y a qué edad puedes conducir?
> – Para sacar el carnet, para conducir un coche, tienes que tener 18 años. Pero puedes conducir una moto de hasta 75 centímetros cúbicos a los

> 16 años. Los de 14 años tienen derecho a conducir un ciclomotor que tiene un motor de un máximo de 50 cc.
> – ¿Y si cometes un delito?
> – Si cometes un delito, a partir de los 16 años compareces delante del tribunal como cualquier ciudadano. Ya eres plenamente responsable bajo la ley. Antes de los 16 años hay tribunales especiales para menores. Si quieres intervenir como testigo, tienes que tener 14 años.
> – ¿Y la mayoría de edad es a los 18 años?
> – Sí. A los 18 años ya puedes abrir una cuenta en el banco, abrir un negocio. Desde los 16 años ya puedes trabajar, pero a los 18 no necesitas que tus padres te den permiso.

Answers:

14 years old: conducir un ciclomotor; ser testigo.
16 years old: conducir una moto; comparecer ante un tribunal; trabajar con el permiso de los padres
18 years old: conducir un coche; trabajar; beber alcohol; abrir una cuenta bancaria

1c Students discuss the similarities and differences between their own country and Spain using the phrases given.

2a Students read the list of worries faced by the Spanish youth and decide which are the ones that worry them and why, and list them according to their own priorities.

2b Students share their list with their colleagues and discuss any differences.

2c Students choose the topic that worries them the most and prepare a presentation explaining the reasons why, and give proposed solutions.

3a Students read the article and compare their answers to exercises 2a and 2b to those given about Spanish young people. They then discuss similarities, differences and potential reasons for these.

3b Students take a stand on a debate about living at home with parents until the age of 30. If the whole class is against, divide the class into two. Each half must defend a position.

Técnica

Filling gaps. Ask students to read this section before they complete activity 4.

4 Students choose the correct answer for each sentence.

Answers:

1 *c*   2 *a*   3 *c*   4 *a*

Gramática

The subjunctive in other past tenses: the perfect and pluperfect subjunctives. Refer students to the relevant grammar section of the Students' Book and the Grammar Workbook.

Answers:

A

1 *Es un milagro que el banco le haya prestado el dinero.*
2 *Me sorprende que se hayan ido de vacaciones.*
3 *Es increíble que no haya causado un accidente.*
4 *Vendrá cuando haya terminado su trabajo.*
5 *Si no hubiese llovido, hubiese venido a la fiesta.*

5a Encourage a brief discussion about young people and citizenship. Is their opinion that the young are good citizens? What do they consider a good citizen? Then students must decide which of the characteristics that follow would be displayed by an ordinary citizen or a good citizen.

Suggested answers:

ordinario, buen ciudadano, ordinario, ordinario, buen ciudadano

 5b Students then listen and compare their answers with those of the recording.

 5c Students listen again for detail and note an example for each of the actions from 5a.

P 65, actividad 5b

Ser buen ciudadano no sólo significa respetar la ley: eso es lo que se espera de todos los miembros de la sociedad.
Un buen ciudadano no es aquel que paga sus impuestos a tiempo; el que respeta los semáforos; no es el que asiste al servicio religioso; el que evita molestar a los vecinos con el ruido de la radio. Tampoco es el que vota en las elecciones. Todo eso se espera del ciudadano ordinario.
El título de "Buen Ciudadano" implica que sea un ciudadano *activo*.
No basta con no ensuciar, sino recoger al menos un papel que no haya tirado. El ciudadano ejemplar no sólo no ensucia, sino que también limpia.
El buen ciudadano da parte de su tiempo a la comunidad: ayuda a aprender a leer a sus conciudadanos, o limpia un área pública, ayuda en la biblioteca, participa activamente en campañas sociales. Tiene la ilusión de construir una sociedad mejor para todos sus miembros.

Answers:

1 *evitar molestar a los vecinos con el ruido de la radio*

2 *ayudar a aprender a leer a sus conciudadanos; limpiar un área pública; ayudar en la biblioteca; participar activamente en campañas sociales*
3 *respetar los semáforos*
4 *votar en las elecciones*
5 *recoger un papel que no haya tirado*

5d Students write an article about the prescribed title. Encourage students to be creative and imaginative.

Gramática en acción

Resources
♦ Students' Book page 66

Answers:

A

1 *hiciese / hiciera*
2 *fuese / fuera*
3 *estudiase / estudiara*
4 *suspendiese / suspendiera*
5 *pudiese / pudiera*
6 *tuviese / tuviera*

B

1 *Mum asked me not to do overtime the day before the exam.*
2 *I hoped the exam would be easier.*
3 *Mum wanted me to study the day before the exam.*
4 *I hoped that I would not fail the politics exam.*
5 *I wish I could catch the train.*
6 *Mum treats me as if I was were still eight years old.*

C

There is more than one logical way of ordering the sentences. It will depend upon the paragraph that the students produce.

D

Carolina tenía el pelo largo, rubio y rizado. Fue a la peluquería y le dijo al peluquero que le cortase el cabello. Emilio, el peluquero, le sugerió que cambiase el color de su pelo. Carolina siempre había querido que su pelo fuese diferente. Siempre había querido parecerse a Victoria Beckham. Decidió que quería tener el pelo corto, oscuro y liso. Cuatro horas después de que entrase en la peluquería, salió una mujer diferente.

E

Students describe their ideal partner practising constructions with the imperfect subjunctive.

F

2, 3, 8

A escoger

Resources

♦ Students' Book page 67

1 Explain to students that Spanish speakers use a lot of idioms, expressions and proverbs in colloquial conversation. Some do have an English translation, for example: *a caballo regalado no le mires el dentado* = never look a gift horse in the mouth. But others do not translate well.

Students try to work out the meaning of common idioms and expressions from the context.

Answers:
1 *b* **2** *f* **3** *a* **4** *e* **5** *d* **6** *c*

2a Students read the text and list the positive and negative aspects of computer games.

2b They design a leaflet to promote the responsible use of computer games.

Repaso Unidades 3–4

Resources

♦ Students' Book pages 68 and 69
♦ CD 2, tracks 8–9

1a Students read the article for gist and briefly discuss what it is about.

Some examples of acceptable answers would be:
A scheme to get teenagers off the streets by involving them in music.
A successful South American / Venezuelan initiative to bring music to the poor.

1b Students read the article, this time for detail, and then they answer the questions.

Answers:
1 *Acercar la música a los niños menos afortunados para darles esperanza.*
2 *Un director de orquesta con mucho éxito que hoy lidera la Filarmónica de Los Ángeles.*
3 *Porque fue a través del "Sistema" que empezó a tocar y proviene de una familia pobre, demostrando que no se necesita ser de clase alta para tocar el violín o tener éxito en el mundo de la música.*
4 *Recibe apoyo económico del gobierno / 23 países han inaugurado programas similares.*
5 *El sentimiento de pertenencia a una comunidad / la experiencia del trabajo en equipo / la satisfacción que produce la música.*
6 *Que los programas inaugurados en el resto del mundo tengan tanto éxito como en Venezuela.*

1c In pairs, or small groups, students discuss their opinion about the project and whether they would like to belong to a similar one.

2a Students discuss the place that music has among the young. They should be encouraged to discuss the positive aspects of different topics such as talent contests, fame, technology, and so forth. They should use structures with *lo*, as suggested in the activity.

2b Students should consider the negative aspects of the issues raised in the previous activity, while still focusing on the use of structures with *lo*.

 3a Students listen to the song by the artist David Bisbal and fill in the gaps.

Answers see transcript:

P 68, actividad 3a

Soldado de papel

Hay un lugar donde no hay sol,
sólo dolor sin marcha atrás
ni dirección tienes que luchar
No, no han crecido y ya tienen valor
no han vivido y mueren por error
y su juego lo destruye el fuego
¡Son niños!
¿Quién puso en tus manos odio de regalo?
¿Quién con tanta ira te lastima?
¿Cómo pudo la inocencia convertirse en destrucción?
¿Quién te habrá robado el mundo en un disparo?
¿Quién le puso precio a tu vida?
¿Cómo vive la conciencia con tanto dolor?
Dime quién, cómo y por qué, soldado de papel.

 3b Students listen again to the song and write a short paragraph to explain what the song protests about. Students could / should mention that the song protests against: the use of children as soldiers / children who lose their childhood to armed conflicts / the unnecessary death of children to war conflicts.

4a Students discuss the message of the songs listed. This could be set as a research / writing exercise if preferred.

Some interpretations of the songs may include:
'Earth Song', Michael Jackson: the power of destruction of the human race / the current sorry state of our planet / misguided interests of world leaders / abandonment of God.
'Beautiful', Christina Aguilera: there are different kinds of beauty / it is ok not to go by the standard idea of beauty set by the media / acceptance of own self without need to change to seek acceptance.
'No son of mine', Genesis: child abuse / domestic violence.

4b Students reflect on current music trends and artists and discuss whether there is a particular current song that could be classed as a 'protest' song because it goes beyond the topic of the love between a couple.

5a Students write 150 to 200 words to support, or express their disagreement with the statement given. They should be reminded that their view needs to be justified fully.

5b Students use the essay that they have written in activity 5a as the basis for preparing a speaking presentation of around 2 minutes duration. Students should not read from the essay. Encourage the audience to ask questions about the presentation in order to stimulate further debate.

6a Students read the synopsis and fill in the information required.

Answers:
Título: Volver
Director: Pedro Almodóvar
Género: comedia dramática / drama comedia
Argumento: Se trata de la vida de tres mujeres, una de las cuales muere y empieza a aparecerse a las otras. La película presenta como las otras dos mujeres llevan la muerte de su madre.
Protagonistas: Raimunda (Penélope Cruz), Sole (Lola Dueñas), la madre (Carmen Maura).
Premios: Cinco premios Goyas, premio a la mejor interpretación femenina y al mejor guión en el Festival de Cine de Cannes.

6b Students translate the synopsis of the film into English maintaining a similar register and level of formality.

Model answer:
Written and directed by Pedro Almodóvar, this comic drama is about three generations of women who survive fire, superstition, madness and even death through kindness, lies and an incredible amount of vitality.

They are Raimunda (Penélope Cruz), married to an unemployed labourer and with a teenage daughter (Yohana Cobo); her sister Sole (Lola Dueñas) who works as a hairdresser; and the deceased mother of both (Carmen Maura), who died in a fire and whose spirit appears to the other characters.

In "Volver", dead and alive cohabit as if it were normal, provoking funny situations or others of genuine and intense emotion. It is a film about the culture of death in the region of la Mancha, where death is lived with an admirable candour, as if the dead never actually died.

Winner of five Goya Prizes, nominated for Hollywood Oscars and winner of the prizes for best female interpretation and best script at the Cannes Film Festival, "Volver" reveals a Spain that is spontaneous, fun-loving, intrepid, bound in solidarity and fair-minded.

6c Students use the synopsis of the film *Volver* as a guide to writing a synopsis of their own of the latest film they have seen (or of a chosen film).

7a Students answer and develop the questions verbally.

7b Students write 100 to 150 words to express their views about the place of image in youth culture and how it does / does not influence the behaviour of the young.

 8 Students listen to the report about competition in the fashion industry in Spain and answer the questions.

Answers:
1 *El Corte Inglés es el rival de Zara.*
2 *Sfera (el Corte Inglés) copia el modelo de Zara; quiere hacerse con el 3% del mercado total; va a abrir 350 tiendas.*

P 69, actividad 8

El Corte Inglés, el gigante español de los grandes almacenes, se ha puesto manos a la obra para plantar cara al fenómeno Zara (Inditex), líder absoluto en el negocio de la moda en España. La estrategia de Sfera (El Corte Inglés) sigue un modelo casi idéntico al de su competidor y pretende hacerse con el tres por ciento del mercado total, gracias al respaldo de Induyco y a su proyecto de abrir 350 tiendas a corto plazo.

Unidad 5 El deporte

Unit objectives

By the end of this unit students will be able to:

♦ Talk and write about traditional and 'fun' sports
♦ Discuss the links between physical exercise and health
♦ Talk and write about different sports personalities
♦ Discuss reasons for taking part in sport and the Olympics

Grammar

By the end of this unit students will be able to:

♦ Avoid using the passive
♦ Use the future and conditional tenses
♦ Use the subjunctive after *cuando*
♦ Extend their use of adverbs
♦ Use *por* and *para* correctly
♦ Use the auxiliary *haber* in a variety of tenses and moods

Skills

By the end of this unit students will be able to:

♦ Employ discussion tactics and structure an argument

Resources

♦ Students' Book pages 70–71
♦ CD 2, track 10

1 Students study the photos and match them to the named sports without looking up words in a dictionary. They try to make intelligent guesses about words they do not recognise and only then do they look up words in a dictionary.

Answers:

1 C	2 E	3 A	4 H	5 D	6 F
7 I	8 G	9 B	10 J		

2 Students try to complete the quiz on their own and then could compare answers with a partner.

Answers:

1 *students' own choice*   2 *students' own choice*
3 *un concurso de ciclismo;   cada septiembre*
4 *b*   5 *c*   6 *2006*   7 *c*
8 *a Severiano Ballesteros   b José María Olazabal
c Sergio García*   9 *Fernando Alonso*   10 *cinco*

3 Students write down three sports for each category. This can be done as a competition with the whole class or individually.

 4a Students listen and decide which sport is being described.

P 71, actividad 4a

1
– Se juega en el agua; se necesita un pádel; se practica todo el año; se puede llevar casco por seguridad.

2
– También se juega en el agua; se practica en el fondo del mar; se necesita un casco y tubos para respirar de un tanque de oxígeno; se lleva un traje de neopreno o buzo.

3
– Se practica en el aire; se necesita mucho valor; se lleva casco de seguridad; se lanzan desde lo alto; se cae por el aire atado a un paracaídas.

4
– Se juega en el gimnasio; se practica en parejas; se lleva un traje protector y un casco; se necesita una espada larga y fina; gana la persona que recibe menos toques en el cuerpo.

5
– Se hacen piruetas y saltos o ses practica a la carrera; se necesitan unos patines y botas; se practica sobre una pista de hielo; gana quien llega primero a la meta o la persona que mejor representa su ejercicio.

Answers:

1 *kayak* 2 *buceo* 3 *parapente* 4 *esgrima*
5 *patinaje sobre el hielo*

4b Students look at the drawings and describe the sport. A partner has to guess which sport is being described. They continue this idea by making up more invented sport such as robot racing or spider fencing.

Tradición contra novedad

Grammar focus

♦ Using *se* to avoid the passive
♦ Future and conditional tenses

Skills focus

♦ Asking questions using *se*

Key language

*se juega, se necesita, se lanza, se ha hecho,
se golpea, equipo, pelota, la pista, se pierden
puntos, marcar, la red, concurso*

Resources

♦ Students' Book pages 72–73
♦ CD 2, track 11
♦ Hojas 21, 24
♦ Grammar Workbook pages 48, 62

1a Students read the texts and decide which of the sports they refer to.

Answers:

1 *torobul*   **2** *levantamiento de piedras*   **3** *jai alai*

1b Now they read the texts again for more detail and find the definitions.

Answers:

1 *all three*   **2** *1*   **3** *1 and 3*   **4** *2 and 3*   **5** *3*   **6** *1*

2a Students listen out for the three modern sports.

P 72, actividad 2a

1

Es un deporte que se juega mucho en Europa, pero no tanto en Inglaterra. Se juega con dos equipos de siete, en un recinto cubierto o en la playa. Se utiliza un balón un poco más pequeño que el balón de fútbol, que no se puede tocar con el pie. Se pueden dar tres pasos con el balón en las manos, y sólo se puede tener el balón durante tres segundos como máximo. Se marca un gol cuando el balón entra en la portería.

2

Es un deporte que se ha hecho muy popular en España a causa del éxito que han tenido Miguel Indurain, Óscar Freire y Alberto Contador. Se puede practicar a nivel individual, pero es más normal hacerse socio de un club. Se practica al aire libre, en carreteras o a veces en pistas especiales. Practicando este deporte se alcanzan excelentes niveles de condición física. En concursos o carreras, se trata de completar el recorrido más rápido que los demás.

3

Se juega con dos o cuatro jugadores. La pelota se golpea con una raqueta pequeña. No se ganan puntos cuando la pelota cae al suelo o da en la red. Es un juego que se practica en el interior y en una mesa.

Answers:

1 *balonmano*   **2** *ciclismo*   **3** *ping-pong*

2b Students listen again for the words given.

Answers:

team – *equipo*   goal – *gol*   small ball – *pelota*
inside – *en el interior*   outside – *al aire libre*
racquet – *una raqueta*   large ball – *un balón*
track – *la pista*   win points – *se ganan puntos*
steps – *pasos*   competition – *concurso*
net – *la red*   to score – *marcar*   race – *la carrera*

Gramática

♦ Students read through the advice about asking questions using *se*.

A They practise asking questions using the prompts provided.

3a Students read the text on kite surfing and try to put into practice the reading skills they learnt in Unit 2. They should try to complete the task without resorting to a dictionary as far as possible. They find the phrases and words in the text.

Answers:

1 *cada vez más sensacionales*   **2** *ya se han inventado*
3 *el vuelo de cometa*   **4** *el deporte de moda*
5 *no es sorprendente*   **6** *se ha vuelto tan popular*

3b Students match the two halves to make a complete sentence.

Answers:

1 *b*   **2** *d*   **3** *a*   **4** *c*

3c Students choose a traditional and a modern sport and write about them.

3d Students then present one of their sports to a partner who guesses the name of it.

Gramática

The future and conditional tenses.

Students read through the section.

A They write out definitions for each of the tenses.

B They could check their answers at the back of the Students' Book to encourage them to find out information for themselves and to get used to using the grammar section for reference.

Answers:

tenga, iré, haré, me gustaría, viviré, saldré, vuelva, descansaré, tendría, leería

C They invent a sport for the future and describe it using only the future tense.

Mente sana, cuerpo sano

Grammar focus

♦ Adverbs
♦ *por* and *para*

Skills focus

♦ Asking questions
♦ Giving advice

Key language

el baloncesto, las ruedas, el aro, la liga, tener suerte, tengo la intención de, cuento con, yo que tú, te aconsejo que, sería mejor que

Resources

- Students' Book pages 74 and 75
- CD 2, track 12
- Grammar Workbook pages 14, 19

1 Students read the text on Juan Rentería and answer the question.

Answer:

SR = en silla de ruedas (wheelchair basketball)

2a Students answer the questions from the text.

Answers:

1 *Terminamos en tercer lugar.*

2 *Se juega sentado.*

3 *Pues, claro un poco porque me gustaría ganar la liga.*

4 *A 3,05 metros* 5 *en un campamento de verano*

6 *porque tendría que viajar y entrenar mucho*

7 *No tanto – ¡este año voy a hacer buceo!*

2b They then practise the interview in pairs, taking the parts of the interviewer and Juan Rentería.

2c Students answer the questions and then discuss their answers with a partner.

2d Students imagine that they are Juan Rentería and write a few thoughts about the future using the *frases clave* provided as prompts.

Gramática

Adverbs.

Tell students to revise how to form adverbs and note the points made.

A When they have completed activity 3a they re-unite the advice using different types of adverbs / adverbial expressions.

3a Students read the advice about maintaining a balance in lifestyles. They then decide an order of importance for each statement.

3b They write down advice for a partner using the prompts provided. These cover the conditional tense, the present subjunctive and the past subjunctive.

 4 Students listen and note down the activities each person does. They list them as sport or relaxation.

P 75, actividad 4

– Hemos preguntado a varias personas acerca de lo que hacen como deporte o para relajarse.

1 Yo soy Ana y me gusta hacer gimnasia; sobre todo aerobic porque me relaja todo el cuerpo y al mismo tiempo afina los músculos. Me siento mil veces mejor después de pasar media hora en el gimnasio.

2 Me llamo Felipe y no hago mucho deporte porque no tengo tiempo después de la oficina y

---

el camino a casa. Prefiero poner la tele y pasar un buen rato viendo programas simples para no tener que pensar en nada.

3 Pues yo, María Elena, voy a menudo a clase de yoga. Me calma la mente y desaparece todo el estrés del día, necesario porque llevo una vida constantemente agitada; es un deporte y al mismo tiempo una diversión que relaja.

4 A mí, Sarita, me encanta correr tres o cuatro kilómetros antes de desayunar; me gustaría hacer más pero no tengo tiempo salvo en los fines de semana cuando hago 10 o más kilometros. Despeja la cabeza y al mismo tiempo me ayuda a pensar y organizar lo que tengo que hacer durante el resto del día.

5 Me llamo Carlos 'el gordito' y voy tres veces a la semana a bailar salsa porque me divierto y hago ejercicio que lo necesito bastante. Antes no hacía nada más que comer golosinas delante de la tele pero ahora el baile me ha salvado y voy bajando kilos poco a poco.

Answers:

1 *aerbic – relajamiento* 2 *ver la tele – diversión*

3 *yoga – relajamiento y diversión*

4 *correr – relajamiento* 5 *bailar salsa – éjercicio y diversión*

Gramática

por and *para*.

Students read through the section and could offer examples for each of the points made.

A They read the text about marathon running and note each example of the usage of *por* and *para* and then translate each one.

Answers:

el por qué y para qué – *the why and wherefore;*

por el cual – *along which;*

para conseguir subir – *to manage to climb onto;*

por minuto – *a minute;*

por agotarse – *about to expire;*

para finalizar – *in order to finish*

5 Students answer the questions in their own words. They could discuss each question as a whole class to help give them more ideas.

La personalidad deportista

Grammar focus

- Compound tenses using *haber*

Skills focus

- Asking questions

Key language

se jacta, se añada, la remuneración, el concenso es, el apoyo, alucinante, tambalea, decaer, el espiral, para abajo, la discapacidad, alcanzar, la cima

Resources

♦ Students' Book pages 76–77
♦ CD 2, track 13
♦ Hoja 22
♦ Grammar Workbook page 38

1a See how many faces students can recognise immediately.

1b and **1c** Students then read the fragments of a newspaper article and match them to the appropriate sports person. Note that this activity could be continued as homework.

Answers:

1 *A*   2 *C*   3 *D*   4 *B*

 2a Students listen to the profile of Seve Ballesteros and complete his personal information form.

P 76, actividad 2a

– El golf es su vida. Gracias a este cantábrico, devoto de su familia e hijo de campesinos humildes, el golf de España se ha convertido en un fenómeno internacional. Nacido en 1957, empezó como *caddie* para los ricos en el club de golf de su pueblo natal, Pedreña (Cantabria), donde aún vive con sus tres hijos y su mujer Carmen. Siempre aseguraba que nunca se retiraría pero ya se jubiló. Nunca olvidará su primer gran éxito en Inglaterra en 1976. Su manera de ser es sosegada, amable, natural y, si no está compitiendo, está jugando, haciendo que otros jueguen o comentando campeonatos para la BBC de Londres en inglés. Dice que la felicidad es el equilibrio; está en el respeto, en la tolerancia y en la comprensión de la gente y así trata de vivir su vida. Sobre todo dice que el deporte hay que hacerlo con moderación; si no, llega a ser insano como el ciclismo en las Vueltas. Este es otro deporte que le gusta muchísimo pero no lo practica como lo hacen los deportistas famosos. Para él es el simple placer de moverse lentamente por los caminos cantábricos, mirando las vistas increíbles del paisaje. Severiano Ballesteros ha hecho por el golf lo que Indurain y Pedro Delgado hicieron por el ciclismo.

2b They listen a second time and make notes in order to write a brief resumé in Spanish.

2c Students research details about another sportsperson from a Spanish-speaking country and present them to the rest of the class orally. Remind them about the work they did on oral presentations in Unit 3. They should try to choose different people so as to gain as wide a panorama as possible.

Gramática

Compound tenses using the auxiliary *haber*. Students read the information and complete tasks A, B and C.

C

Answers:

1 *present subjunctive – future perfect:* When you see me I will have completed the triathlon.
2 *preterite – conditional perfect:* I thought you would have chosen a different type of exercise.
3 *perfect:* I have lost my glasses! Where have I put them?
4 *pluperfect:* Pepe had come back before Jorge.
5 *pluperfect subjunctive – imperfect – conditional perfect:* If I had known it was going to rain, I would not have gone out.

3a Students read the introduction about Oscar Pistorius the Blade Runner. They match up the questions with an appropriate answer.

Answers:

1 *c*   2 *f*   3 *h*   4 *d*   5 *a*   6 *b*   7 *e*   8 *b*

3b Students then practise making this into an interview.

4 Students read the article about the state of sport today and answer the questions in their own words but basing their answers on the text.

Suggested answers should contain:

1 *España tiene muchos deportistas famosos*
2 *porque ganan mucho dinero y están en la tele y en revistas*
3 *que hay muchos y dan un buen ejemplo*
4 *es una situación triste*
5 *Students' own words and ideas*
6 *Students write 200 words to express their own opinions on the state of sport today.*

Mundiales y Olímpicos

Skills focus

♦ Debating, discussing and structuring an argument

Key language

el legado, el coste, heredar, hospedar, los inconvenientes, vale la pena, un escaparate, quitar las ganas, darse cuenta de que, un certamen, en cuanto a

Resources

♦ Students' Book pages 78 and 79
♦ CD 2, track 14
♦ Hojas 23, 25

1 Students listen to the points of view about hosting the Olympic Games. They note down the order in which they hear each comment. It would help students to look through the statements first.

P 78, actividad 1a

- A ver, Marco, tú estarías de acuerdo con que los Juegos Olímpicos se celebraran en nuestro país?
- Pues, a mí me parece que por una parte sí sería buena idea por lo que queda después pero por otra parte también comprendo los argumentos en contra porque es verdad que necesitamos hospitales y colegios.
- Vale. Entonces explica primero cuáles son los inconvenientes.
- Lo que más me preocupa es el coste. Creo que va a aumentar demasiado y que al final seremos nosotros los que tendremos que pagar.
- Vaya, ¡qué ideas tan negativas! Cualquier dinero que se gaste estará bien gastado porque se van a construir muchos edificios bonitos y útiles y después todos podremos usar estas facilidades.
- Lo que pasa es que los arquitectos quieren tener toda la gloria y a veces construyen edificios impresionantes pero poco prácticos.
- Bueno, vamos a concentrarnos en los juegos. Alfredo, ¿tú tienes una opinión sobre lo que atrae del deporte?
- Claro que sí. En mi opinión, verlo es una parte esencial del deporte. Los mejores del mundo necesitan los campeonatos para demostrar su excelencia. Además, a nosotros los espectadores nos encanta verlos. Es un espectáculo que verdaderamente vale la pena.
- En cuanto al deporte comprendo que es un escaparate para el élite del deporte pero mi pregunta es si de verdad anima a los jóvenes a participar en el deporte o si les quita las ganas.
- A fin de cuentas si quieren triunfar tienen que darse cuenta de que hay que hacer un esfuerzo en la vida. De nada les sirve pensar que todo se puede alcanzar sin moverse del sofá.
- En conclusión al mismo tiempo que produce negocio y atrae turistas y su dinero, también cuesta mucho construir y preparar un certamen como los Juegos Olímpicos o cualquier Copa Mundial. Por supuesto hay muchos a favor y muchos en contra.

Answers:

D   J   B   E   L   I   F   A   K   G   H   C

1b   For each point of view students decide whether it is favourable or not.

1c   Encourage students to add their own points of view.

1d   Students should then respond to the points of view expressed.

1e   In pairs, they discuss the question: 'What use are national and international competitions?'

Técnica

Students read through this section carefully. Ask them for their reactions and also ask them to give examples of their own.

A useful extension task could be to revisit the previous units and note examples for discussion on the topics. This could be used as a way of revising previous topics.

2   Students read the text about the Americas Cup and answer the three questions, using the text as a basis for their answers, but also thinking about the whole unit.

Answers should contain:
1 énfasis en lo negativo   2 and 3 – students' own thoughts and ideas

3   Students read the two texts about women in sport, focusing especially on the Olympics.

4   They discuss the points raised, and then have a whole class debate on the motion:

'The male chauvinist attitude in sport is conspiring to keep sport in the Stone Age'.

Gramática en acción

Resources
♦ Students' Book page 80

Students complete the reminders about *por* and *para*. They use the grammar section of the Students' Book to confirm their answers.

A   Students write out the sentences correctly.

Answers:
1 *por*   **2** *para*   **3** *para*   **4** *para*   **5** *para*

B   They write six more sentences to show the use of each of *por* and *para*.

C   Student A gives a verb of action such as *correr – corrió*, and then student B responds with an appropriate adverb to say how the action was completed: *rápidamente* or *rápido*.

Students remind themselves about all the compound tenses using *haber* that they have covered so far.

D and **E**   They read the text and note the tenses using *haber*. They analyse each one indicating the tense.

Answers:
1 se han enfrentado – *perfect reflexive*
2 había atraído– *pluperfect*
3 han tenido que – *perfect*
4 se había preparado – *pluperfect reflexive*

5 ha sabido – *perfect*

6 no le ha gustado – *perfect*

7 *se* haya recuperado, haya podido – *perfect subjunctive*

8 haber ganado – *perfect infinitive*

9 había hecho – *pluperfect*

F Students re-use all the tenses identified in the text above and make up an imaginary story. This could be done orally as a shaggy dog story with each student making up a sentence and adding it to the previous one.

A escoger

Resources

♦ Students' Book page 81

♦ CD 2, track 15

 1a Students listen and note down the ideas expressed about bullfighting. They present these as opinions using the *frases clave* as prompts.

P 81, actividad 1a

– Cada año matan a miles de toros.

– La corrida es cruel y denigrante.

– Los que viven en las ciudades llevan una vida desconectada de la naturaleza.

– Podemos apreciar las corridas de toros como parte de nuestra historia, pero no como parte de nuestra cultura.

– Las corridas de toros son un símbolo de la cultura española.

– En el ruedo, el toro es más peligroso que el hombre, pero el hombre lo domina.

– La corrida sobrevive como espectáculo de una forma de vida que ha desaparecido.

– En España el fútbol es más popular que los toros.

– Los toros no tienen relevancia en una sociedad moderna como España.

1b Students read the text about bullfighting and respond to the attitudes expressed. They also then decide if they agree or not with the last statement.

1c Students read the bullfighting phrases and then apply them in the sentence frames following the example.

Answers:

Students should use the following expressions.

1 *lidiar*   **2** *echarse al ruedo*

3 *saltarse a la torera*   **4** *la puntilla*

1d Students revise page 78 on debating and formulating an argument and prepare a debate on the motion 'Blood sports have no part to play in society today'.

2 Students read the short text about Hawk Eye and prepare a short essay on why such devices are necessary in sporting competitions today.

Unidad 6 ¡Salud!

Unit objectives

By the end of this unit students will be able to:
- Relate modern lifestyles to health
- Analyse government health campaigns
- Discuss the problems of addiction
- Consider the ingredients of a healthy life

Grammar

By the end of this unit, students will be able to:
- Use the perfect infinitive
- Use the subjunctive for doubt or improbability
- Use demonstrative adjectives and pronouns
- Use the imperfect continuous
- Use indirect speech

Skills

By the end of this unit students will be able to:
- Use different strategies when listening for detail
- Pinpoint information in a text
- Write a summary in English

Conductores distraidos

Resources
- Students' Book pages 82 and 83
- CD 2, tracks 16–17

1a By way of an introduction to the unit, students work in pairs and study the information and pinpoint the various stages of dangers of alcohol.

1b They categorise two aspects for each stage.

 1c Students listen and check their answers.

P 82, actividad 1c

La primera etapa es la de riesgo. El conductor se siente emocional, excitado y empieza a perder la capacidad de juicio.
Sigue la etapa de alarma. El conductor pierde la inhibición, y se vuelve impulsivo, incluso agresivo.
La tercera etapa es cuando se vuelve peligroso conducir. El conductor ya no tiene control preciso de sus movimientos, sus reacciones se han debilitado y no percibe el peligro de su situación.
La etapa de conducción más peligrosa es cuando empieza a ver doble y la confusión es total.
Finalmente, resulta imposible conducir a consecuencia del efecto narcótico que lleva al estupor o incluso al estado de coma.

Answers:
etapa de riesgo 1+3; *etapa de alarma* 4 + 10;
peligroso conducir 6 + 7; *sumamente peligroso de conducir* 8 + 9; *imposible de conducir* 2 + 5

2 Students study the cartoon and decide what the problem is.

Answers:
El hombre dice que el conductor es muy sensato porque sólo bebe agua, pero es un perro y su dueño está tan borracho que le deja conducir.

3a Students study the images and in pairs explain what each one is about.

 3b Students listen and put the images in order, according to what they hear.

P 83, actividad 3c

- ¿Así que no debemos fumar y conducir a la vez?
- No exactamente, pero el tabaquismo se considera como un factor importante en los accidentes de tráfico. Los fumadores tienen un riesgo 1,5 veces más alto en comparación con los conductores no fumadores.
- ¿Cómo se explica ese hecho extraordinario?
- Pues, se han propuesto varias razones. En primer lugar, fumar puede tener un efecto tóxico, debido al monóxido de carbono o a la nicotina. Luego se dice que el conductor puede distraerse en el acto de encender un cigarrillo.
- ¿Entonces sí que deberíamos prohibir que los conductores fumen?
- Creo que en muchos casos el riesgo resulta del hecho de fumar en general, no de fumar mientras se conduce. El tabaquismo se asocia con enfermedades como las enfermedades cardiovasculares, el cáncer... lo que significa que el conductor fumador tiene peor estado de salud que otros conductores. Y tal vez también intervienen factores de la personalidad, si los fumadores son más propensos a aceptar un comportamiento arriesgado.
- ¿Es realmente un problema grave?
- Se cree que un 5% de los accidentes de tráfico se atribuyen al hecho de fumar en el interior del vehículo.

Answers:
A B D C

 3c Students listen a second time and complete the sentences.

Suggested answers:

1 *El riesgo que corren los fumadores es **1,5 veces más alto**.*

2 *En primer lugar, fumar puede tener **un efecto tóxico**.*

3 *Además también el conductor puede distraerse **en el acto de encender un cigarrillo**.*

4 *En muchos casos el riesgo resulta del **hecho de fumar en general**.*

5 *Un 5% de los accidentes se atribuye **al fumar**.*

3d In pairs, students explain the problems and their causes to each other.

3e Students write a notice warning of the risks of smoking while driving.

El alcohol

Grammar focus
♦ The perfect infinitive

Skills focus
♦ Listening for detail

Key language
al haber bebido;   de haber bebido;
después de haber bebido;   debe haber;
deberían haber;   de haberlo sabido;
el botellón;   podría haber

Resources
♦ Students' Book pages 84 and 85
♦ CD 2, track 18
♦ Hoja 26
♦ Grammar Workbook page 66

1a Students read the publicity leaflet *¡Vive!* and identify in which section the four ideas listed are expressed.

Answers:

1 *3rd paragraph*	2 *1st paragraph*
3 *2nd paragraph*	4 *1st and last lines*

1b Then they identify positive and negative imperatives. To refresh their memory, they can revise the Gramática box on page 34.

Answers:

positive: *evita, reflexiona, piensa, bebe, olvídate, párate*

negative: *no conduzcas, no te montes, no participes*

1c Students read the sentences and decide which text they belong to: *¡Vive!* or *Vida*.

Answers:

1 *Vida* 2 *¡Vive!* 3 *Vida* 4 *Vida*
5 *¡Vive!* 6 own choice

1d Students compare the health warning with the advertisement and decide which of the two would have most impact on young people.

1e Students use the *frases clave* and the information from the advertisement *¡Vive!* to criticise the advertisement *Vida*.

Gramática

The perfect infinitive.
Remind students how to form the perfect and pluperfect tenses. Then take them through the steps for forming and using the perfect infinitive. Ask them to give further examples of their own to compare the English and Spanish translations: gerund – perfect infinitive.

A Students translate the sentences into English.

Answers:

1 *Rafa said he had put his seatbelt on.*

2 *If I had known, I would not have got into the car.*

3 *I/He/She should have gone to my house in a taxi.*

4 *Having drunk he should not have driven.*

B Students use the perfect infinitive to translate the sentences into Spanish.

Answers:

1 *Haber bebido tanto fue mala idea.*

2 *Haber conducido a casa fue muy peligroso.*

3 *Al haber llegado a la casa, se acostó.*

4 *Debe haber bebido agua.*

Técnica

Listening for detail.

Students read through this advice and add it to the advice already given in unit 1.

 2 Students listen and choose the correct ending.

P 85, actividad 2

– Al haberse prohibido en muchas ciudades, el botellón ya no es el fenómeno que era hace unos años. Los padres y los vecinos han podido caracterizar a los jóvenes de borrachos, fuera de control. Miguel, de 15 años, nos explica qué significa "botellón".

– Se junta un grupo de jóvenes, todos ponen dinero, y compran bebidas alcohólicas en una tienda o supermercado. Luego beben las bebidas en la calle y montan una fiesta. Tal vez es porque es muy caro beber en un bar. Muchas veces son jóvenes menores de edad, que no pueden entrar en los bares o discotecas.

– Los jóvenes dicen que no hay alternativas suficientes. Elena, de 16 años, nos ha comentado:

– Querríamos tener un sitio donde reunirnos, algún centro nocturno donde pudiéramos decidir cómo divertirnos con responsabilidad. Las

---

> únicas opciones "legítimas" cuestan dinero: ir al cine o a un bar. Las autoridades deberían haber pensado en cómo darnos las instalaciones que necesitamos.

Answers:
1 *a* 2 *b* 3 *b* 4 *a*

3 Students write statements for and against the statement.

Las adicciones

Grammar focus
♦ The subjunctive: doubt and improbability

Key language
los drogadictos; actuar; picarse; el toxicómano; drogarse; perjudicar; detener; castigar; la dependencia; dudo que; es poco probable que; una campaña de publicidad

Resources
♦ Students' Book pages 86 and 87
♦ CD 2, track 19
♦ Hojas 27, 29, 30
♦ Grammar Workbook page 55

1a Students read the article and decide who says each of the statements.

Answers:
Irma Sánchez: 2, 4, 7; Iván Gómez: 1, 3, 5, 6

1b, 1c Students decide which aspects they agree with and write them out following the example.

They then write down the conclusions they have come to, starting the sentences with *Creo que ....*

Gramática

Subjunctive of doubt and improbability.

Ask students to read the grammar box and then to give examples of their own in English to ensure they have grasped the main subtleties of the usage.

1d Students write out sentences to say which sentiments they do not agree with using verbs in the subjunctive and the *frases clave*.

2a Students read the opinions 1–8 about smoking and decide which ones agree to government intervention.

Answers:
3, 7, 8

2b Then they match the statements a–h to the opinions 1–8.

Answers:
a *2* b *4* c *5* d *1* e *7* f *3* g *8* h *6*

3a Students listen to Inma, Pili and Mateo and decide if they are for or against the ban on cigarette smoking in public places.

P 87, actividad 3a

Inma
Mi abuelo fumaba y murió de un cáncer de pulmón, pero no creo que prohibir el tabaco sea la respuesta. Si todos tenemos la información necesaria, cada uno puede decidir si quiere fumar o no.

Pili
Lo que más me escandaliza es que las compañías inciten a los jóvenes a fumar. Casi nadie empieza a fumar a los veinticinco o treinta años. Y la mayoría de los que fuman quieren dejarlo. Debería ser ilegal, no sólo fumar en lugares públicos sino también el vender cigarrillos a los menores de 30 años.

Mateo
La prohibición sólo hace que fumar sea más atractivo para algunos jóvenes que no quieren conformarse. Lo que deberían prohibir es la publicidad del tabaco en todos los países del mundo.

Answers:
Inma – No; Pili – Sí; Mateo – No

3b In conversation with each other, students explain their own feelings on the subject.

3c Students write a paragraph giving arguments for and against the banning of smoking in public places.

Salud es vida

Grammar focus
♦ Demonstrative adjectives and pronouns

Skills focus
♦ Pinpointing information

Key language
saludable; legumbres; grasas; gozar de; verduras; fruta; el equilibrio; carecer de; nivel de vida; relajarse; el estrés

Resources
♦ Students' Book pages 88 and 89
♦ CD 2, track 20
♦ Hoja 28
♦ Grammar Workbook page 13

1a Students follow the tasks to help them understand the text.

1b Students find information in the text to complete the chart.

1c Students use the information gathered to answer the question 'Is the Spanish diet healthy?'

Técnica

Pinpointing information.

Students read the advice and then use the steps to help them understand the text *Comer para vivir. Vivir para comer.*

Gramática

Demonstrative adjectives and pronouns.

This consolidates grammar that students will have learnt previously.

A Refer students to the text on page 88 from which they make a list of the demonstrative adjectives and pronouns, and qualify them.

Answers:
ese *fenómeno = adjective, masculine singular*
éste *es el secreto = pronoun, masculine singular*
Este *descubrimiento = adjective, masculine singular*
esta *dieta = feminine singular*
aquellos *dulces = (those) adjective, masculine plural*
estas *costumbres = adjective, feminine plural*

B Get students to explain the differences in nuances of meaning between the adjectives and pronouns in their list.

Answers:
There are no absolute right/wrong answers. The important thing is to have looked through the text five times. Rather than getting students to write answers down, get them to tell a partner. Give them oral feedback.

2a Students read the text ¿*Cómo aprovechar la vida?* and pinpoint ways of saying the phrases 1–6 in Spanish.

Answers:
1 *siempre querer tener más*
2 *No olvides la importenía del tiempo libre.*
3 *El secreto es mantener el equilibrio.*
4 *No busques el estres adicional.*
5 *La publicidad nos ofrece cada vez más productos seductores.*
6 *La sobrecarga de trabajo nos quita tiempo.*

2b Point out that the ideas in the phrases 1–4 are mixed up. The task is to correct them.

Answers:
1 *En el trabajo evita una agenda atestada.*
2 *En el tiempo libre evita obsesionarte.*
3 *Durante el dia reserva tiempo para descansar.*
4 *Con la familia aprovecha el tiempo juntos.*

2c Get students to look for examples in the text of how to enjoy life.

Possible answers:
divide el día en tres: dormir, relajar, trabajar;
mantener el equilibrio;
no llenar tu agenda – citas / compromisos sociales / deportes;
decir no al consumismo

 3a Students listen to Maritza and complete the chart as indicated.

Tareas	Actividades	Descanso
14 ticks	*5 ticks*	*6 ticks*

P 89, actividad 3a

El despertador suena a las siete. Despierto a mi hija mayor, Ruth, que tiene trece años y se arregla sola para ir al instituto. Más tarde despierto a mi hija pequeña, Nieves, y después de desayunar, vamos caminando al colegio.
No vuelvo a casa, sino que hago las compras para el día.
Llego a casa a las diez y media, y empiezo mis tareas: limpiar, cocinar, lavar, planchar, coser, bricolaje ... A veces escucho la radio, pero luego me enfada.
Si viene mi marido a casa, comemos a las dos y media.
Por la tarde, después de recoger la cocina, tengo tiempo para mirar catálogos o hacer compras en Internet.
Luego tengo que recoger a mis hijas y preparar su merienda. Si ven la televisión puedo hacer aerobic. Luego hacen los deberes y yo preparo la cena. A las ocho las niñas se bañan.
Cuando llega mi marido, cenamos, y después recogemos la mesa todos juntos.
Ruth y Nieves se acuestan a las diez, y empieza la parte más tranquila del día. Hablo con mi marido, leo o veo la tele. Luego me acuesto y a medianoche apago la luz y me quedo dormida.

3b In pairs, students describe a typical day in their lives including work (*el trabajo*), leisure (*el ocio*), ways of relaxation (*el descanso*) and meals (*la comida*).

Una vida "Zen"

Grammar focus

♦ The imperfect continuous
♦ Indirect speech

Skills focus

♦ Writing a summary in English

Key language

sentirse bien; trabajando; durmiendo; poniendo; aguantar; ignorar; los beneficios

Resources

- ♦ Students' Book pages 90 and 91
- ♦ CD 2, track 21
- ♦ Hoja 30
- ♦ Grammar Workbook pages 43, 46

1a Students read the three texts and decide for which person each category is the most important.

Answers:

1 *Lety* **2** *Sofía* **3** *Mariano* **4** *Sofía* **5** *Mariano*

 1b Students listen to the recording and decide who is speaking, Lety or Sofía.

P 90, actividad 1b

1

El secreto es no exagerar. Es importante no abusar de tu cuerpo, pero tampoco perder la perspectiva de la vida normal. Yo no como mucha carne, pero no soy vegetariana. Hago ejercicio y tengo una dieta muy equilibrada, pero lo más importante es estar a gusto. No tengo filosofía ni doctrina. La vida es para disfrutarla.

2

Puedes comer bien y estar en forma, pero si no encuentras tu camino, estás perdido. Debes buscar la satisfacción dentro de tu propio ser, no en factores exteriores. Eso me costó muchos años entenderlo.

Answers:

1 – *Lety* **2** – *Sofía*

1c In pairs, students explain to each other which of the categories in exercise 1a are the most important for them.

1d Ask students to outline the profile of a person who gives no thought to diet, exercise or identity.

Gramática

The imperfect continuous.
Students read through the grammar information. Ask them to give examples of their own in English to highlight the similarities with the structure in English

A Students re-read the text on page 90 and translate all the examples of the imperfect continuous they can find.

Answers:

estaba trabajando *(I was working)*

estaba viviendo *(I was living)*

(estaba) durmiendo *(I was sleeping)*

me estaba poniendo *(I was making myself)*

Estaba ignorando *(I was ignoring)*

estaba viviendo *(I was living)*

Estaba buscando *(I was looking for)*

B Students rewrite the underlined parts of the sentences 1–3 in the imperfect continuous.

Answers:

1 *Estaba estudiando* **2** *Estaba visitando*
3 *Estaba buscando*

Indirect speech.
Students read the information and then practise putting examples into indirect speech and give examples of their own.

A

1 *Dijo que no se complicaba la vida pero sí se cuidaba.*

(*dijo* + imperfect and *dijo* + present can be used too.)

2 *Dijo que se estaba poniendo enfermo y no se daba cuenta* (other tense combinations are possible).

3 *Dijo que había visitado el Japón y la India, que había leído mucho y había pensado sobre ello.*

Técnica

Writing a summary in English.

Students study the strategies given for writing a summary. Take them through each bullet point asking for comments.

Students then complete the tasks A, B and C either individually or as a class, or with a partner.

A Ask students to write one sentence summing up the information about all three people on the previous page.

B Ask students to write one sentence to sum up each person.

C Now students write a full 120-word summary of the experiences of the three people on the previous page. They should focus on how their lives have changed.

Gramática en acción

Resources

- ♦ Students' Book page 92

Students revise each grammar point and complete the tasks.

The perfect infinitive

Revise the rules for the perfect infinitive.

A Students should decide whether the past participle should change or not.

Answers:

1 *no change* **2** *change to* bebidos
3 *change to* herida **4** *no change* **5** accidentados

B Students write a list of consequences for each picture to tell a story.

The subjunctive for doubt

Use of the subjunctive for expressions of doubt

C Students complete the sentences putting the verbs into the subjunctive.

Answers:

1 *sean* **2** *deba* **3** *contribuya* **4** *tenga* **5** *esté*

D Students give their own opinions remembering to change the verb into the subjunctive mood if using a phrase of doubt or improbability.

The imperfect continuous

Remind students they can use *estaba* + present participle to make the continuous form of the imperfect.

E Tell students to imagine they have had an accident. They must explain to the doctor what they were doing and what happened to them.

A escoger

Resources

♦ Students' Book page 93

1 Students read the text about organic food and answer the questions in their own words.

2 Students write a letter (150 words) to the imaginary person giving advice and asking questions.

3 Students look at the carton and answer the questions.

4 Students answer the questions in their own words.

Repaso Unidades 5–6

Resources

♦ Students' Book pages 94 and 95
♦ CD 2, track 22

1a Students read the text and categorise points a–g. The categories are:

1 properties of energy drinks

2 properties of isotonic drinks

3 not mentioned in the text

Answers:

a *i* **b** *i* **c** *i* **d** *iii* **e** *i* **f** *i* **g** *ii*

1b Students write a résumé of the text in 100 words.

2 Students study the advertisement and describe it in their own words by answering the questions.

3 Students read the text and choose the most appropriate answer.

Answers:

1 *a;* **2** *a;* **3** *b;* **4** *a;* **5** *c*

 4 Students listen to the recording and answer the questions in Spanish.

> P 95, actividad 4
>
> – No sólo es importante qué ejercicio hacemos, sino con qué frecuencia lo practicamos. Si el ejercicio más popular es andar, ¿con qué frecuencia se practica?
> – Pues, es la más popular, y de lejos la forma de ejercicio más frecuente. De los que afirman andar, el 75% lo hace a diario, y otro 14% tres o cuatro veces por semana.
> – Así que la mayoría lo practica a diario. ¿Pasa lo mismo con ir al gimnasio o correr?
> – Ir al gimnasio es más popular que correr, pero se practica con menos frecuencia. De los que van al gimnasio, sólo 24% lo hacen a diario, cuando el 29% de los que corren lo hacen cada día. La natación se practica de manera aun menos frecuente y otros deportes raramente se practican más de dos veces a la semana.

Answers:

1 *el andar* **2** *el 89%* **3** *ir al gimnasio*
4 *el correr* **5** *la natación* **6** *dos veces a la semana*

5 Students study the graph and answer the questions in their own words orally.

Unidad 7 Haciendo turismo

Unit objectives

By the end of this unit students will be able to:
- Describe some tourist destinations in the Spanish-speaking world
- Discuss different types of holidays
- Consider the impact of tourism on countries and local communities
- Examine the environmental effects of travel and tourism
- Compare opinions on climate change

Grammar

By the end of this unit students will be able to:
- Use cardinal numbers
- Use constructions with *si*
- Use continuous tenses
- Use impersonal verbs in reflexive expressions
- Use the passive

Skills

By the end of this unit students will be able to:
- Recognise and use different registers of language
- Write a formal letter
- Use a monolingual dictionary
- Organise ideas and facts in order to plan a piece of written work

Resources
- Students' Book pages 96 and 97
- CD 2, tracks 23 and 24

1a Students list Spanish-speaking countries.

Answers:
Bolivia, Perú, Paraguay, Chile, Argentina, Puerto Rico, Costa Rica, Panamá, Colombia, Cuba, Ecuador, República Dominicana, El Salvador, México, Guatemala, Nicaragua, Honduras, Uruguay, Venezuela

1b Students may already know one or two of the destinations and may be able to work out others using common sense. For example, El Salar de Uyuni – salt, white colour. They then complete and check their answers with listening exercise 2a.

 2a Students listen to the travel agent to complete and check their answers to exercise 1b.

Answers:
1 *B:* Bolivia   2 *C:* México   3 *D:* Chile   4 *A:* Perú

P 96, actividad 2a

Bueno, ¿qué les recomendaría que visitaran en América Latina? Pues, Perú es un destino muy popular porque lo tiene todo: cultura, selva amazónica y, por supuesto, el Machu Picchu y la Ciudad Perdida. Machu Picchu es probablemente el símbolo más conocido del imperio inca y es la atracción turística más visitada y la que genera más ingresos en el país.

También recomiendo una visita a Bolivia que, aunque tiene muchos parecidos con Perú por su cercanía, tiene lugares únicos y fascinantes como, por ejemplo, el Salar de Uyuni: en la distancia parece nieve, pero es la llanura de sal más grande del mundo. Se extiende 10.582 km^2, si no me equivoco, y se puede visitar en coches 4x4, pero se debe ir siempre acompañado por un guía para no perderse. Los turistas más aventureros se alojan en alguno de los hoteles de sal, que son fascinantes porque tanto el edificio como el mobiliario están totalmente construidos de sal.

Claro, que si buscan unas vacaciones más convencionales un destino muy popular es México donde, aparte de las zonas costeras, se pueden visitar algunos lugares de interés histórico como las ruinas de las pirámides de Chichén Itzá que fueron construidas por la civilización maya y atraen muchísimos turistas que visitan Latinoamérica.

Hmmm … ¿Algo más relajante y tranquilo? Hmmmm … Déjenme pensar … Si buscan una combinación de relax y herencia histórica … Sí, ¡por supuesto! La chilena Isla de Pascua, en el Océano Pacífico. ¿Han oído hablar de los Moais? ¿No? Bueno, los Moais son más de 600 estatuas gigantes de piedra monolítica que se encuentran distribuidas por toda la Isla de Pascua. Su significado es incierto y hay muchas teorías sobre su origen.

 2b Students listen to the recording again and then answer the questions.

Answers:
1 *Porque es la atracción turística que genera más ingresos*
2 *Están completamente construidos de sal*
3 *Los maya*   4 *el océano Pacífico*   5 *600*

3 Students work independently and then collaboratively to see how much they know about Latin America.

Answers:

1 *b*	2 *a*	3 *c*	4 *a*	5 *c*
6 *b*	7 *a*	8 *b*	9 *c*	10 *b*

4a Students listen for the correct number that completes the sentence.

P 97, actividad 4a

1 España tiene 40 millones de habitantes y mide 504.749 km^2 incluyendo a Baleares y Canarias.

2 Andalucia tiene 7.357.558 habitantes y es la Comunidad Autónoma más grande de España.

3 La Comunidad de Madrid tiene una extensión de 8030 km^2.

4 El pico de Mulhacén tiene una altura de 3.482 metros.

5 Dicen que hay 360 días de sol en la Costa del Sol.

6 Cada año llegan más de 50 millones de turistas a España.

7 Por muchas razones el año 1992 fue un año clave.

8 España tiene una media de 650 metros de altura siendo el segundo país más alto de Europa después de Suiza.

9 Madrid – Magherib en árabe – fue nombrada la capital en 1561.

10 Las cuevas de Altamira datan de 18.000 años antes de Cristo.

Answers:

a *40* **b** *504.749* **c** *7.357.558* **d** *8.030* **e** *3.482*
f *360* **g** *50 millones* **h** *1992* **i** *650* **j** *segundo*
k *1561* **l** *18.000*

4b In this activity, students have the opportunity to share their experience of Spain, or other Spanish-speaking countries with the rest of the class. If their experiences are limited, encourage them to explain which country they would like to visit, and say what attracts them to it.

¡Merecidas vacaciones!

Grammar focus

♦ Constructions using *si*

Skills focus

♦ Different registers of language

Resources

♦ Students' Book pages 98–99
♦ CD 2, tracks 25–26
♦ Grammar Workbook page 58

1a Students read the advert on page 98, and make a list of the activities that are mentioned in it.

1b Students then practise speaking by choosing a destination mentioned that they would be interested in visiting. They must also practise the ways of expressing opinions in the *frases clave*.

1c Students team up in pairs and interview their partner about his / her own preferences. Encourage them to use the vocabulary from the *frases clave* in their questions.

1d Students listen to the tourists speaking, and work out what part of the country they have been visiting according to the advertisement *¡Ven a España!*

Answers:
1 *Asturias* **2** *Alicante* **3** *Islas Canarias* **4** *Galicia*

P 98, actividad 1d

1 Bueno, en mi opinión la relación calidad–precio es excelente. El hotel era un poco caro pero había gran variedad de tratamientos de belleza para escoger y los masajistas tenían mucha experiencia y eran muy agradables. Es un placer alojarse allí y descansar de los estreses de la vida cotidiana.

2 ¡Fué fantástico! ¡No os podéis creer la variedad de actividades alucinantes que había! Lo más increíble fue el descenso a los barrancos. ¡Cómo mola, tío!

3 Les llamo para expresar mi desagrado en relación con mi reciente estancia en su hotel. Cuando hice la reserva se me aseguró que el hotel estaba muy bien situado en un lugar idóneo para dejar que los niños se bañasen sin peligro. La realidad es que la cercanía del club náutico suponía un riesgo constante.

4 Pasar las vacaciones borracho, yendo de una discoteca a otra me parece una vergüenza. Yo he utilizado mis vacaciones para relajarme y admirar la belleza natural del país. Debemos aprender a apreciar y proteger los recursos naturales.

Técnica

A Students describe what they think of the advertisement *¡Ven a España!* taking into account the information given in the Técnica box.

B Students go on to discuss how different kinds of publicity attract the attention of different kinds of people.

C Students choose the adjectives that they feel best describe the advertisement. Encourage them to choose carefully and be able to justify their answers.

D They listen to the touristss again and describe the kina of language they use.

Gramática

A Students read the sentences and by referring to the explanations in the Gramática box, decide why certain tenses have been used.

Answers:

1 *The subjunctive is used because it refers to an unlikely situation (to be famous)*

2 *The imperfect indicative is used because the* si *clause expresses the idea of 'whenever', in the past.*

3 *The conditional is used because it is impossible, or doubtful, that the action referred to can take place.*

B Students decide what would be the most appropriate tense to complete the sentence in each case.

Answers:

1 *puedes* **2** *fuéramos* **3** *hubiese resultado*

C Students use the sentences in the article on the previous page in conjunction with the explanations in the *Gramática* box to write their own sentences using the *si* structure.

3 Students look at the photograph and discuss what they see among themselves. There are no right or wrong answers but students must be encouraged to justify their answers.

4a Students listen to the programme and note down the required information.

P 99, actividad 4a

Perú, oficialmente conocido como la República de Perú, está en el oeste de Sudamérica. Es un país de contrastes, tiene regiones de selva, costa y las cordilleras montañosas de los Andes. En el norte, comparte sus fronteras con Ecuador y Colombia y en el sur tiene frontera con Chile. Los 2.414 kms de costa peruana es bañada por el Océano Pacífico, mientras que al este se encuentran Bolivia y Brasil. En total este sorprendente país se extiende 1.285.220 km², unas dos terceras partes de la extensión total de México, lo que lo coloca en el lugar número veinte del ránking mundial de países según su extensión. Su sistema gubernamental es la república constitucional, donde los ciudadanos eligen al presidente y éste selecciona al primer ministro para que le apoye en su tarea.

Indios americanos habitaron las tierras de Perú durante milenios, pero hoy en día sus más de 28 millones de habitantes son de etnias y orígenes muy variados, el resultado de los cinco siglos de historia que comenzaron con la conquista española en el siglo XVI.

El español es la lengua más hablada y la lengua materna de la mayoría de los jóvenes, pero coexiste con multitud de idiomas indígenas, el más importante de los cuales es el quechua, que es hablado por un 16% de la población. La capital de Perú es Lima, que es la ciudad con mayor densidad de población del país, en la que se concentran unos ocho millones de

---

ciudadanos. Otras ciudades importantes son Arequipa, Trujillo, Chiclayo y Cuzco.
La economía del país es moderada, con ingresos per cápita de poco más de 280 dólares al mes, y aunque industrias como la pesca, la agricultura, la minería y los textiles crean empleo, todavía se considera que más del 50% de la población vive en la pobreza. Perú tiene moneda propia, el Nuevo Sol.
Perú es sin duda un país de contrastes, y la carencia de medios económicos coincide con la riqueza de su cultura en la que las celebraciones y tradiciones indígenas se unen a las de la religión católica que domina un país rico en música, danzas, artesanía y gastronomía popular, ingredientes de un folklore únicamente exquisito y abundante.

Answers:

Gobierno: república constitucional
Superficie y comparación: 1.285.220 km², 2/3 de México, 20. país más grande del mundo
Población y habitantes: variada, 28 millones
Capital y ciudades importantes: Lima (capital), Arequipa, Trujillo, Chiclayo y Cuzco
Industria: pesca, agricultura, minería y textiles
Cultura: celebraciones y tradiciones indígenas, religión católica, música, danzas, artesanía y gastronomía popular
Otro: Idiomas: español y quechua.
Moneda: Nuevo Sol

4b Students revise the Técnica section and listen again if needed to decide what kind of language is used in the report. A variety of answers may be acceptable providing that they can justify their answer. The more appropriate answers would include *serio*, *formal* and *objetivo*.

5 In this activity, students must do their own research on a Latin American destination of their choice to produce a factual article. Then they need to adapt the facts and the language to produce an advertisement with the objective of attracting tourists to their destination.

El turismo significa dinero

Grammar focus
♦ Continuous tenses

Skills focus
♦ How to write formal letters

Resources
♦ Students' Book pages 100–101

+ Students' Book pages 100–101
+ CD 2, tracks 27–28
+ Hojas 31, 32, 34
+ Grammar Workbook page 43

1a Students read the 10 effects of tourism given and decide if they are positive or negative.

Answers:
Positive: 1, 3, 4, 6, 8
Negative: 2, 5, 7, 9, 10

1b Following on from activity 1a, students try to think of any other effects of tourism to discuss.

 2a Students listen to Ramón and decide what is his overall opinion of tourism.

P 100, actividad 2a

El turismo tiene un lugar importantísimo en mi vida, pues llevo trabajando tres veranos en un cámping, lo que me ha permitido continuar mis estudios.
Además, me está ayudando muchísimo con el inglés. Hablo todos los días con los visitantes y hablar inglés es una ventaja en el mundo laboral.
Personalmente, trabajar en la industria del turismo también me está animando a viajar. No pienso pasarme la vida aquí, pero para viajar tengo que estudiar, aprender más idiomas y conseguir un buen trabajo.
A mi edad, mi abuelo estaba trabajando todo el día en el campo pero yo puedo combinar mi trabajo con los estudios.
Con el dinero que está generando el turismo, se están mejorando el transporte, los restaurantes, los centros recreativos y el patrimonio cultural e histórico de la zona.

Answer:
Positive

 2b Students listen to the recording again and work out which points are <u>not</u> mentioned.

Answer:
4 and 6

 3a Students listen to Jessica's presentation and again decide if her opinion of tourism is positive or negative.

Answer:
Negative

P 100, actividad 3a

Mi presentación: El turismo en España.

El turismo en España tiene muchos aspectos que tenemos que considerar. Tal vez el más obvio sea el desarrollo económico. España ocupa el segundo lugar mundial en ingresos

---

procedentes del turismo, alcanzando los €40 billones anuales. El único inconveniente es que otros sectores de la economía no han tenido el mismo éxito. El turismo ha afectado al medio ambiente. Imagínate una isla como Menorca donde viven cien mil habitantes, pero que recibe cada verano seis millones de visitantes. No llega el agua, no hay donde tirar la basura. El litoral se llena de hoteles. Afortunadamente, el turismo masivo se limita a la costa.
Con la construcción de hoteles, los precios de los terrenos y de las casas se vuelven desorbitados. Los jóvenes que encuentran trabajo en los centros turísticos tienen grandes dificultades en encontrar vivienda.
El comportamiento de los extranjeros no siempre responde a las expectativas de los españoles, pero su influencia se siente en los cambios sociales que se han experimentado recientemente. El horario de las comidas, la dieta, el alcohol, la libertad sexual, todos han ido contagiando las costumbres tradicionales.
Los turistas tratan España no como un país donde viven 40 millones de personas con una historia, una cultura y un estilo de vida, sino como un lugar geográfico con sol y playas. No debemos permitir que España se reduzca a un parque temático artificial.

 3b Students listen again and make a list of points mentioned by Jessica.

Answers:
Some examples may include:
Desarrollo económico
Efecto nocivo en el medio ambiente
Turismo masivo en la costa
Incremento de los precios de la vivienda
Cambios del comportamiento social
Percepción geográfica – no humana – del país

Gramática

Continuous tenses. Students read the notes on the formation and uses of the tenses.

A They listen to Ramón again and note down the continuous tenses he uses.

Técnica

How to write formal letters. Students read the eight points and look for examples in the letter opposite.

4a Students read the letter and find as many instances of continuous tenses as they can. There are eight examples.

4b Students translate the letter with the use of a dictionary if needed. Although word by word (literal) translation should not be encouraged, the translation must carry the same level of formality as the original.

4c Students now reply to the letter. Encourage different levels of detail depending on the ability of the students. But again, it must be a formal letter.

Un mundo más pequeño

Grammar focus

♦ Use of impersonal verbs

Skills focus

♦ Using a monolingual dictionary

Key language

charlar por los codos
llamar al pan, pan y al vino, vino
llevarse como el perro y el gato

Resources

♦ Students' Book pages 102–103
♦ CD 2, track 29
♦ Hojas 33, 35
♦ Grammar Workbook page 63

1a Students name the airlines that they have used. Encourage discussion / debate on the subject of budget airlines v. regular airlines.

1b Students use the context of the article to find the words and expressions required.

Answers:

1 *aerolínea*	2 *aeronaves*	3 *hoy en día*
4 *sobrepasa*	5 *de bajo coste*	6 *éxito*
7 *despegó*	8 *asequibles*	9 *principales*
10 *puntuales*		

1c Students in pairs discuss the advantages and disadvantages of budget airlines.

2 Students listen to the article and answer the questions:

P 103, actividad 2

La coordinadora de Colectivos Ciclistas de Aragón ha convocado una jornada para reivindicar la vulnerabilidad de los ciclistas en las calles frente a los conductores de otros vehículos.
En nuestras ciudades llenas de contaminación y atascos, utilizar la bici para las tareas diarias, como ir al trabajo, no es solamente el método más rápido, sino que también es la manera más racional de moverse en las ciudades.
Las peticiones de los participantes son muy claras: que se reduzca el excesivo uso del coche y de esta manera, sus efectos nocivos sobre la ciudad, sus habitantes y el medio ambiente, y también que haya justicia en las

---

calles: menos protagonismo del automóvil y más ayudas a alternativas como el transporte público, caminar y, por supuesto, la bicicleta. De lo que se trata, es de promocionar una movilidad sostenible como solución al tráfico colapsado de las ciudades.
La marcha tuvo lugar en varias provincias españolas y otras ciudades de Europa y el mundo.

Answers:

1 *La vulnerabilidad de los ciclistas frente a conductores de otros vehículos*
2 *Es el método más rápido y más racional.*
3 *Reducir el excesivo uso del coche, justicia en las calles*
4 *La promoción de la movilidad sostenible para solucionar los problemas de tráfico*
5 *Varias españolas y provináas europeas ciudades*

Gramática

A Students read the article in activity 1 again and focus on trying to spot the impersonal verbs used.

B From the article students have just listened to, they make some sentences of their own using the impersonal expressions given.

3a Students reflect on the occasions when they have travelled by car in the last three days and list them with the day, distance and reason for travel. If students have not been in a car, the time span can be increased or the exercise can focus on a member of their family instead.

3b Students reflect upon the real need to use the car on each of the occasions mentioned in activity 3a and as a class exercise, they debate the issue together. Prompt your students to think of alternatives such as public transport, the possibility of combining journeys and other similar suggestions.

Técnica

A Students use a monolingual dictionary to find out the meaning of some of the words mentioned above. Some students may already be familiar with some of the meanings so you may need to be selective when you choose which words they should look up.

B Students try to work out the meaning of the Spanish colloquial idioms by use of translation and common sense.

Answers:

charlar por los codos = to be a chatterbox
llamar al pan, pan y al vino, vino = to call things by their name (to call a spade a spade)
llevarse como el perro y el gato = not to get along, to argue all the time (to fight like cat and dog)

4a Students read the newspaper headlines and discuss what they are about.

4b Following on from the discussion in activity 4a, explain to students that in Spain there are certain weekends every year that tend to be peak accident weekends. This is mainly because a high percentage of Spaniards take their holidays at the same time, generally during the months of July or August. Most head for the coast for the duration, thus creating massive queues and causing many accidents on specific weekends. A similar situation can occur at Easter, and occasionally in the festive season. These peak traffic dates are referred to as *Operación salida* and *Operación retorno*.

Then the students express their opinion on the Spanish holiday system and its traffic problems, and compare it to their own country.

4c Students choose a newspaper headline and write a fictitious article using appropriate reporting language that should include the use of some impersonal verbs.

El cambio climático

Grammar focus

♦ Passive structures

Skills focus

♦ Organising ideas and facts for a structured written response

Resources

♦ Students' Book pages 104–105
♦ CD 2, track 30
♦ Grammar Workbook page 62

1a Students have to think about their behavioural changes in very hot weather. They should come to the conclusion that more heat equals more energy use from air conditioning units and so on, which adds to environmental pollution and contributes to global warming.

1b Students will have come across most of the vocabulary during their GCSE studies, and they should be able to work out the rest – with some common sense.

Answers:
1 *Climate change*
2 *Melting of the icecaps*
3 *Torrential rain*
4 *Global warming*
5 *Hole on the ozone layer*
6 *Heat wave*
7 *Greenhouse effect*
8 *Drought*
9 *Floods*
10 *Forest fires*

1c Students then think back to when they were younger and discuss what the weather was like then, and if it has changed. They should be encouraged to use the linking expressions in the *frases clave*.

2 Students read the article and choose the three topics relating to environmental problems that are mentioned.

Answers:
Use of energy; recycling of water; environmental pollution

Gramática

A Students look for passive structures in the text and re-write them in the active voice. Remind them that this implies using the reflexive structure in most cases.

Answers:
Los edificios estarán diseñados ... = los edificios se van a diseñar ...
... muchos litros de agua potable pueden ser ahorrados ... = ... pueden ahorrar muchos litros de agua potable ...
... que después de ser depuradas ... = ... que después que se depuren ...
... que está construida sobre los principios ... = ... que se construyó sobre los ...

 3a Students listen to five different opinions and decide where they would place each opinion on the diagram.

Answers:
A *1* **B** *5* **C** *3* **D** *2*

P 105, actividad 3a

1 Definitivamente nosotros somos la causa. La rapidez con que sube la temperatura no tiene precedentes, ni tampoco la tasa en que se incrementa el dióxido de carbono en la atmósfera. Ninguna causa natural es capaz de ocasionar los cambios que estamos experimentando.

2 Yo creo que es el ciclo normal. Sólo hace falta observar las tendencias de otros planetas en el sistema solar: todos los planetas están atravesando una fase más cálida de lo habitual. Sospecho que nuestras emisiones de CO_2 no causan el calentamiento de Marte, ¿no?

3 ¿Culpables o no? ¡Bueno ...! ¡Menuda batalla! Es un proceso natural pero supongo que nosotros no es que ayudemos a frenar el proceso, ¿verdad?

4 Ya a principios del siglo XX se quemaban millones de toneladas de combustibles fósiles. ¿Por qué no se calentaba la Tierra entonces? Y cuando los volcanes entraban en erupción por todo el planeta, los dinosaurios estaban vivos. ¿Había calentamiento global entonces? ¡Los

dinosaurios se murieron de frío! ¡Dejémonos de tonterías! ¡Disfrutemos y pongámonos morenos! Ah ... y ... ¡No compremos los periódicos!

5 Está claro que hay un ciclo climático pero son nuestras acciones las que lo empeoran. Los científicos creen que hay un 90% de posibilidades de que nosotros seamos la causa del calentamiento global. Cuando estamos enfermos, no vamos a un mecánico, ¿no? Entonces no deberíamos preguntar al público general sobre cambios climáticos. Escuchemos a los expertos, ellos saben de lo que hablan.

3b Students listen again to the opinions and choose which speaker it is who mentions, or implies, each of the six statements.

Answers:
a *3*   **b** *5*   **c** *4*   **d** *5*   **e** *1*   **f** *2*

Técnica

Writing skills – organising ideas and facts for a structured response.

Students read through the Técnica box and complete the tasks following the instructions and guidance given.

Here is a suggested plan for 1a:
Introduction explaining car dependency society/excessive car volumes
Advantages of cars: personal / social with justifications
Disadvantages of cars: personal / social with justifications
Alternatives / feasibility of alternatives
Personal experiences or hypothetical situation
Point of view supported and why
Conclusion / closing statement

Gramática en acción

Resources
♦ Students' Book page 106
♦ CD 2, track 31

A Students listen to the recording while looking at the illustration. Then they note down which statements made by Elisenda are not true according to the illustration.

P 106, actividad Gramática actividad A

– Elisenda, ¿has ido a la playa hoy?
– Sí, sí he ido. Estaba llenísima, gente por todas partes, ¡un agobio!
– ¿Algo interesante?
– No, lo de siempre, la verdad: un niño estaba

---

construyendo un castillo de arena, un par de chicas estaban haciendo footing y un bebé estuvo llorando porque se le había caído el chupete y la mamá ... ¡ni caso!

– ¿Estaba la pandilla?
– Sí, estaban jugando al voleibol: chicos contra chicas.
– ¿Y quién ganó?
– No sé. ¡Ah! Y una chiquilla adolescente llena de pecas se estaba embadurnando de crema, parecía que se la regalasen.
– Bueno, lo de siempre, ¿no?
– ¡Ah sí! ¡Qué fuerte! Cuando me iba, un hombre estaba entrando en el agua totalmente desnudo, ¡tal y como vino al mundo!

Answers:
Un niño estaba construyendo un castillo de arena.
Dos chicas estaban haciendo footing.
Chicos contra chicas estaban jugando al voleibol.

B Students correct the false statements according to the illustration.

Answers:
Una niña estaba construyendo un castillo de arena.
Un hombre estaba haciendo footing.
Unos chicos (o dos equipos mixtos) estaban jugando al voleibol.

C Students describe what everyone else in the scene is doing using the imperfect continuous.

D Students practise the use of the continuous tenses and object pronouns by re-writing the sentences following the example.

Answers:
1 *Rita lo está limpiando. Rita está limpiándolo.*
2 *María se lo estaba lavando. María estaba lavándoselo.*
3 *Las estábamos viendo. Estábamos viéndolas.*
4 *Las chicas las están haciendo. Las chicas están haciéndolas.*
5 *Me lo estoy poniendo. Estoy poniéndomelo.*
6 *Nos los estarás diciendo. Estarás diciéndonolos.*

E Students complete the sentences with the conjugated form of the verb in brackets.

Answers:
1 *fuera / gustaría*   2 *pueden / quédense*
3 *pasábamos / tomábamos*   4 *quisiera / conocería*
5 *hubieses visitado / hubieses probado*

A escoger

Resources
♦ Students' Book page 107
♦ CD 2, track 32

1a Students read the article mainly for gist and write a short summary in English.

1b This exercise is dedicated to students' research and independent work. They research the phenomenon of bioluminescence and produce an information leaflet in Spanish to promote ecological tourism. Students should be encouraged to consider all positive and negative aspects of tourism studied during the chapter and to recycle key vocabulary.

 2a Students listen to the radio interview and note down who mentions the various aspects.

P 107, actividad 2a

– Estamos charlando hoy sobre la popularidad de viajar. Miguel, nuestro reportero, ha entrevistado a algunos jóvenes para saber sus opiniones sobre tomar un año de descanso para ver mundo. Escuchemos lo que decía Jesús:
– Pasar un año viajando por el mundo me ha permitido conocer y convivir con culturas diferentes a la mía. Esto me hizo ampliar mi perspectiva como persona. Espero volver a hacerlo algún día.
– Veamos lo que nos contaba Elena:
– Bueno, el mundo no es tan grande como antes. No quiero ponerme a trabajar todavía; voy a estudiar, buscar un empleo a tiempo parcial y quiero viajar. Quiero conocer a gente, tengo que madurar.
– Maite y Eugenia viajaron recientemente. Veamos lo que les pareció la experiencia:
– Esperaba encontrar a otros españoles para no estar sola, pero conocí a un montón de gente de todas partes del mundo. Seguimos en contacto por Internet, y somos muy, muy amigos.
– Fue una experiencia que me hizo crecer como persona y profesionalmente. Me dio la oportunidad de conocer a gente de todo el mundo, de viajar y de divertirme un montón.
– Bueno, y aquí viene lo que le contaba Sergio a nuestro reportero cuando le preguntó sobre sus viajes:
– Cuando vives en un país es muy natural que lo consideres el centro del mundo. Quería dejar atrás mi mundo, separarme de todo lo familiar. Te das cuenta que el mundo que conoces es tu mundo, y sólo tu mundo. Viajar te deja conocer otros mundos, y cuando vuelves, ya eres otro.
– Y por fin, escuchemos lo que nos cuenta Hammú:
– Para mí ha sido una experiencia infinitamente enriquecedora. Me ha permitido crecer como profesional y como persona, y conocer un país realmente atractivo y lleno de contrastes.
– Y tú, ¿qué piensas sobre la idea de tomarse un año para ver mundo? Llámanos al 93 869 82 574 y cuéntanos. ¡Esperamos tu llamada!

Answers:

	Amigos	Desarrollo personal	Divertirse	Trabajo	Estudios
Jesús		✓	✓		
Elena	✓	✓		✓	✓
Maite	✓				
Eugenia	✓	✓	✓		
Sergio		✓			
Hammú		✓			

 2b Students listen again and work out who has not yet travelled.

Answer:

Elena

3a Students discuss if they agree or disagree with the statement and justify their viewpoint.

3b Students use the discussion of the previous activity to produce a formal letter expressing their opinion. Students should be encouraged to follow the guidance on page 105, and they should be reminded of the use of the appropriate language register for this task.

3c Students use the letter that they have written in activity 3b to prepare a brief oral presentation that summarises the main points. Peers should be encouraged to ask questions at the end of the presentation.

Unidad 8 La familia y las relaciones personales

Unit objectives
By the end of this unit students will be able to:
- Examine different types of relationships with family members and friends
- Discuss the values of young people
- Talk about the causes of conflict between generations
- Comment on specific differences between the generations in Spain
- Discuss the importance of marriage and the family in today's society

Grammar
By the end of this unit students will be able to:
- Use exclamations
- Use possessive pronouns
- Use the subjunctive in a broader range of expressions
- Use prepositions correctly

Skills
By the end of this unit students will be able to:
- Adapt information from texts

Situaciones difíciles

Grammar focus
- Exclamations

Key language
romántico, necio, simpático, violento, tierno, impulsivo, antipático

Resources
- Students' Book pages 108 and 109
- CD 2, tracks 33–34
- Grammar Workbook page 14

1a Students work in groups to decide which of the images in their own opinion best fits the situation described.

Answers:
Students' answers will vary.

1b Students choose one of the situations and, changing the first person to the third, write a paragraph explaining what happened and the consequences.

1c In pairs, students prepare and act out one of the situations.

Gramática
Exclamations.
Remind students about exclamation marks and accents.

2 Students write their own exclamatory phrases for each situation.

Possible answers:

¡Qué conejo más lindo! ¡Qué niño tan romántico!
¡Qué tierno! ¡Qué conejo tan travieso!
¡Qué niña tan ingrata!

 3a Students listen to the parents and match each one with one of the situations illustrated.

Answers:
1 *a*   2 *c*   3 *b*

 3b They then listen to the young people and identify which situations they are referring to.

Answers:
Carlos B; José A; Nacha C

P 109, actividad 3a

1 Fuiste a un botellón. Un amigo mío os vio allí, borrachos en la calle. No lo pude creer cuando me lo dijo. Si vas a una fiesta es para divertirte, no simplemente para beber.

2 Ya te dije que no me gusta que tu novio suba a tu dormitorio. Esperaste hasta que yo saliera y le invitaste a subir. Si crees que no me enteré, estás equivocada.

3 Te pusiste las zapatillas de tu hermano. Sabías que las acababa de comprar y que le costaron mucho dinero. Te fuiste todo el día con tus amigos, y él se pasó toda la mañana buscando sus zapatillas.

P 109, actividad 3b

Carlos
Si él siempre se pone mi ropa – cogió mi chaqueta y nadie le dijo nada. Yo tenía prisa, tenía que ir a terminar un trabajo para el instituto. No son los únicos zapatos que tiene. No entiendo por qué se enfadó tanto. ¿Por qué no me llamó al móvil en lugar de perder el tiempo?

José

Lo que pasa es que salí con unos amigos a pasear, eso fue todo. Era tarde, eso sí, pero nadie tenía ganas de volver a casa. Estábamos en un lugar donde hay como una plaza pequeña donde se reúne la gente. Creo que había un café o algo por el estilo, con mesas y todo, pero estaba cerrado. Algunos amigos estaban allí y nos invitaron a tomar una cerveza.

Nacha

No lo hice a propósito. Él vino a la casa porque sabe que no te cae muy bien, y quería hablar contigo. Como tú no estabas, no supe qué hacer. ¿Qué ibas a pensar? Entonces le invité a subir a mi dormitorio – es mi habitación y, al fin y al cabo, no debes decirme lo que puedo y lo que no puedo hacer allí.

Alfonso

Me paso la vida en la calle. Me divierto un montón, y allí somos todos iguales, compartimos todo y hablamos el mismo lenguaje, no como en casa. Hoy en día tenemos muchos tipos de relaciones. Lo más normal es no tomártelas demasiado en serio hasta que conoces a alguien especial.

Salvador

Yo trato siempre de respetar sus límites, sus normas. Llego a la hora, como en casa, no les contesto. Pero no me gusta que me hagan interrogaciones del estilo: "Adónde vas? ¿Con quién andas?". Realmente pasamos muy poco tiempo juntos, y así hay menos roce, menos contacto y menos posibilidad de pelearnos. No digo que nos llevemos mal, sino que sabemos evitar el conflicto.

Virginia

Puedo hablar de casi todo con ellos. A veces no les gusta lo que digo, pero saben que si quiero algo, voy a hacerlo de todas formas. A veces se escandalizan, pero también son comprensivos. Creo que puedo hablar con ellos porque no me ponen límites.

Entenderse con la familia

Grammar focus

♦ Possessive pronouns

Key language

me llevo bien / mal / mejor con ...; discutir a causa de ...; confiar en ...; los bisabuelos; la ciudadana; los conflictos

Resources

♦ Students' Book pages 110 and 111
♦ CD 2, track 35
♦ Hoja 37
♦ Grammar Workbook page 28

 1a Students listen to the discussion between the five young friends and decide whether they are talking about family or friends.

P 110, actividad 1a

Sara

Muchos de ellos no se interesan más que por la ropa y los zapatos. Si quiero hablar de algo serio – de política o de lo que pasa en el mundo – no encuentro a casi nadie de mi edad con quien pueda tener un diálogo inteligente. Soy una persona muy seria y a veces me encuentro muy sola.

Irene

Yo no les digo nada de lo que hago. Si no, discutimos – por las notas, por el sexo, por tonterías. Sé que no les gustaría lo que hago, así que mejor no se lo digo. Es mejor callar que decirles mentiras. No quiero que me pidan explicaciones ni que me hagan reproches. No les pido nada, e insisto en que me dejen en paz.

 1b Students listen a second time and note whether they are positive or negative comments.

Answers:

Sara: *amigos, negativo* Irene: *familia, negativo* Alfonso: *amigos, positivo* Salvador: *familia, más positivo que negativo* Virginia: *familia, positivo*

1c In pairs, students use the *frases clave* to explain to each other how they get on with their family or friends.

2a Students read the text about Montse's family. They match each generation to the appropriate description.

Answers:

1 *sus padres*
2 *los jóvenes de hoy*
3 *sus abuelos*

2b Students decide who is speaking for each of the sentences.

Answers:

1 *su abuelo*
2 *su madre*
3 *Montse*

2c Students back up their answers with evidence from the text.

Gramática

Possessive pronouns.

Students revise possessive pronouns.

Answers:

A

1 *de la mía*

2 *el suyo*

3 *al nuestro*

4 *a la nuestra*

3 Substitute the underlined words with the correct form of the possessive pronoun.

Answers:

1 *la suya*

2 *los suyos*

3 *la suya*

4 *la mía*

5 *la tuya*

4 Students read the card game then make the diamond shape according to the different opinions expressed by the different members of the family. They follow the example to explain why each opinion is in the place they have put it in.

5a Students explain why and how they think that Montse's life is different from that of her parents.

5b Students prepare a debate on the themes.

Amistades y conflictos

Grammar focus
◆ Consolidation of previous grammar from the unit

Skills focus
◆ Adapting information from texts

Key language
*los iconos   la paga   rebelarse   gastar
los piercings   entenderse   los tatuajes
la paradoja*

Resources
◆ Students' Book pages 112 and 113
◆ CD 2, track 36
◆ Hojas 38, 40

1a Students listen to the descriptions and decide which icon is being described.

> P 112, actividad 1a
>
> 1 En mi cumpleaños nunca pido regalos, prefiero que me den dinero.
> 2 No entiendo por qué es aceptable que se ponga un arete, un pendiente o algo en el lóbulo de la oreja pero mis padres se escandalizan si me lo pongo en el ombligo.
> 3 Sé que te hace daño – te lo advierten en el paquete – pero somos lo bastante adultos como para decidir.

> 4 Emborracharse – es normal, ¿no?
> 5 Tu tatuaje es muy bonito, ¿es de verdad? ¿Te dolió mucho?
> 6 Puedo hacer nuevos amigos por el mundo entero y comunicarme con ellos.
> 7 Es el último grito de la moda – tengo que comprar una.
> 8 Siempre estoy en contacto con la pandilla.
> 9 No como en mi casa, pero no paro de comprar chucherías.

Answers:

1 *D*   2 *A*   3 *H*   4 *E*   5 *G*   6 *C*   7 *I*   8 *B*   9 *F*

1b Students read the texts and complete the grid.

Answers:

Los iconos mencionados	El icono más importante	Razones
Héctor *dinero, beber, ropa, tecnología*	*dinero*	*Rebelan contra sus padres, pero no contra la sociedad: el consumismo. Todo lo que hacen para rebelarse cuesta dinero.*
María Elena *ropa, piercings, cigarrillos, móvil*	*móvil*	*Pertenece a los jóvenes. Son muy comunicativos.*
Marco Antonio *dulces, tatuajes, piercings*	*dulces / chucherías*	*Para recordar que son niños. No quieren hacer lo que les mandan, pero no quieren actuar como adultos responsables.*

Técnica
Adapting information from texts.
Students read this boxed information and complete the tasks.

A Students practise organizing information taken from a text. Help them separate a list of points taken from the text into ideas and examples, taking care to avoid giving conflicting points of view. Different answers are possible. For example, *la tecnología* could be considered as an example.

Possible answers:

Ideas: *la rebeldía   la tecnología   la comunicación   el consumismo*

Examples: *el alcohol   el tabaco   el móvil   la ropa   Internet   los dulces   el dinero   los tatuajes*

B Students read the examples and complete the grid.

Answers:

Algunos dirían que …	Pero se podría decir que …
los jóvenes no quieren que les traten como niños.	los jóvenes no quieren actuar como adultos.
los jóvenes quieren tomar sus propias decisiones.	los jóvenes no quieren que les digan qué tienen que hacer.
los jóvenes quieren rebelarse.	los jóvenes son muy conscientes de su imagen y quieren sentir que pertenecen a un grupo y no son diferentes de los demás.

C and **D** Students complete the tasks using their own words and examples.

Example answers (D):

1 *A los jóvenes no les interesa trabajar.*
2 *A los jóvenes les importa mucho impresionar a sus amigos.*
3 *A los jóvenes les fascina la moda.*

El matrimonio

Grammar focus

♦ Further uses of the subjunctive

Key language

soportar divorciarse separarse pelearse sobrellevar el intermediario el autoestima es imprescindible que los recién casados disculpar

Resources

♦ Students' Book pages 114 and 115
♦ CD 2, track 37
♦ Grammar Workbook page 55

1a Students read the texts on divorce and search for the meaning of the words in the list.

Answers:

se vuelven / se convierten en   acaban / terminan
requiere / necesita   soportar / adaptarte
jamás / nunca   te hace falta / debes
una fase / una etapa   motivo / causa
aconsejamos / recomendamos

1b Students decide which of the two texts includes each statement.

Answers:

1 *1 5 8*
2 *2 3 4 6 7*

1c Students choose the most important points to advise the two people.

Gramática

Further uses of the subjunctive.
Students read this information. Ask them to give further examples of their own in English.

A Students give the grammatical explanation for the uses of the subjunctive in these sentences.

Answers:

1 possibility
2 impossibility
3 emotion / value judgement
4 value judgement
5 not wanting
6 improbability

B Students complete the sentences using ideas from the texts.

2a Students read the text *Consejos para los recién casados* and list the positive and negative imperatives.

2b Students find similar ways of giving each command.

2c Students use their imagination and write the letter of advice as if they were a grandparent.

 3a Students listen to the recording and make notes.

P 115, actividad 3a

Mónica
Mis padres se separaron y yo empecé a portarme muy mal, les hacía sufrir mucho. A mi madre le decía cosas horribles. Le echaba la culpa de que iba a suspender mis exámenes y al final dejé de estudiar.

Edgar
Después del fin de semana, que pasaba en casa de mi papá, mi madre me sometía a un interrogatorio. Me preguntaba cómo era la nueva novia de papá, si tenían lavaplatos o si salían de copas por la noche. Quería saberlo todo.

Inma
Mi papá siempre tenía mejores cosas que hacer que prestarme atención. Llegaba tarde a casa, cuando yo ya había preparado la cena en lugar de ver la tele. Tampoco había hecho los deberes.

3b Students explain to a partner the situation regarding one of the young people.

La familia y la realidad

Grammar
♦ Prepositions

Key language
alguien   novio   la pareja   preocuparse de / por
mudarse   salir del armario   flipar atropellarse
compartir   alcanzar   ahorrar

Resources
♦ Students' Book pages 116 and 117
♦ CD 2, track 38
♦ Hojas 36, 39
♦ Grammar Workbook page 18

1 Students read the texts and say to whom the sentences refer: Joaquín, José, Ana, or Leila.

Answers:
  1 *José*
  2 *Joaquín*
  3 *Ana*
  4 *Leila*
  5 *José*
  6 *Joaquín*
  7 *Ana*
  8 *Leila*
  9 *Ana*
  10 *Leila*

Gramática

Prepositions.
Students will need time to look through all the examples.

A Students identify the preposition and explain its use in the examples.

  2 *de* usually means 'of' or 'from' but here means 'out of';

  3 *de* – as before but here means 'about';

  4 *al* usually means 'at', but here means 'on the edge of' (idiomatic expression);

  5 *en* usually means 'in' but here means 'on which' (needed in Spanish but not in English);

  6 *de* usually means 'from', but here means 'of' (different word order in English);

  7 *a* usually means 'at', but here is used as the personal *a* (note no need for 'for' in 'to look for');

  8 *de* usually means 'of' or 'from', and here is used to mean 'possession of my parents' [house] (different word order in English);

  9 *para* usually means 'in order to' / 'for'; here means 'to get married';

  10 *de* usually means 'for' or 'from' , but here means 'that'.

2 Students learn to evaluate each other's responses to key questions on the unit.

3 Students listen to Freddy's response and evaluate it.

P 117, actividad 3

– ¿El matrimonio es importante?
– Pues, yo creo que las relaciones personales son más importantes que el hecho de casarse. Vivir solo … tener pareja … encontrar a alguien que te quiera …: todas estas circunstancias son posibles, y no quiero decir que una sea mejor que otra. Creo que es importante pensar bien en si vas a tener hijos, teniendo en cuenta las responsabilidades que conlleva, y que no lo hagas sin pensar. Pero casarse no significa automáticamente que vayas a ser un buen padre, y divorciarse tampoco implica que seas un ogro …

Example answers:

Ideas, opinions, relevance (10)	Fluency, spontaneity (10)	Range of language (5)
A high mark	A high mark	A high mark
Thinking on his feet, but following an idea through logically, looking at things from different points of view.	Thinks on his feet, uses strategies to give himself time. Good use of sentence starters, gives reaction then digs out a justification.	Clearly focused on slipping in subjunctive. Good use of sentence starters, opinions etc. Sentences with "if". He knows it is an assessment situation and has made sure he puts in language that will help get a good mark.

4 Students write a response to the key question.

Gramática en acción

Resources
♦ Students' Book page 118
Students revise each grammar point then complete the tasks.

A Students identify the subjunctive in the sentences and explain why it is being used in each one.

Answers:

1 doubt

2 wanting

3 impossibility

4 emotion

B Students make sentences, changing the verb to the subjunctive.

Example answers:

Quiero que mi padre vaya a pagar el móvil; No creo que sea mi verdadero padre; Dudo que mis padres puedan vivir juntos; / Es imposible que mi madre tenga un nuevo novio; Es ridículo que mis padres me regañen

C Students provide subjunctives to improve Rosa's sentences.

Example answers:

– *¿Existe un modelo típico de familia?*

– *No creo que exista. Es importante que los individuos decidan cómo quieren vivir.*

– *¿La familia tradicional va a desaparecer?*

– *No, no es probable que desaparezca. Pero podemos impedir que su importancia disminuya.*

D Students translate the megative imperatives.

Answers:

1 *No te preocupes.*

2 *No llores.*

3 *No te vayas.*

4 *No lo lleve.*

E Students suggest what they would say to the people in the illustrations.

Possible answers:

A *No le eches agua.*

B *No nades aquí.*

C *No copies.*

D *No lo compres.*

F Students explain, using the subjunctive, why the people in pictures A, B, C and D should take their advice.

Possible answers:

Es peligroso que nades porque es probable que te coma un tiburón.

No es justo que copies porque no quiero que saques mejoras notas que yo.

Es importante que no compres este coche porque dudo que funcione.

A escoger

Resources

♦ Students' Book page 119

♦ CD 2, track 39

1 Students listen to the recording and decide which person is making the complaint.

> P 119, actividad 1
> – En el programa de hoy tenemos dos jovencitos, jóvenes y guapos los dos, que se casaron hace un año y no dejan ya de pelear. Lupita, Lupita, Lupita, ¿qué os pasa, eh?
> – Hola, ¿sabes qué? Me trata como su madre. Tengo que aguantar que llegue tarde sin avisar, y si le pregunto de dónde viene ... ¡hmm! Tengo que hacer las compras, cocinar, hacer las camas, todo ... y eso cuando trabajo más que él. Y gano más. A veces creo que eso es parte de su problema.
> – Creo que tenemos que conocer a Rogelio. Rogelio, por favor ...
> – Tú siempre quieres saber todo lo que hago, pero cuando llego a casa, casi nunca estás. Trabajas hasta las nueve de la noche, y no te voy a estar esperando en casa como un mono, como un angelito, viendo la televisión. ¡Te diré dónde voy, si quieres! Voy a la casa de mi mamá para comer algo sabrosito y caliente.
> – Rogelio, aquí tenemos a tu madre, que te tiene algo que decir, muchachón ...

Answers:

1 *Rogelio*

2 *Rogelio*

3 *Lupita*

4 *Lupita*

5 *Lupita*

6 *Rogelio*

2 Students prepare a similar radio programme in which they and their parents confront each other. They use the situations from page 108 to base their work on.

3a Students read the text and complete a grid.

Answers:

1 *4, 9* 2 *3, 11, 12, 13* 3 *5, 14* 4 *8*
5 *6, 7* 6 *1, 2 ,10* 7 *9*

3b Students continue the idea and invent more examples of their own.

Repaso Unidades 7–8

Resources

♦ Students' Book pages 120 and 121

♦ CD 2, tracks 40–41

1a Students read the text and match up the two halves of the sentences according to the information given in the text for those wanting to get married.

Answers:

1 *f*   2 *g*   3 *i*   4 *c*   5 *a*

6 *e*   7 *h*   8 *d*   9 *b*

1b Students answer the questions in their own words and explain their reasons orally.

2 Students listen to the recording and decide which of the phrases are mentioned.

P 120, actividad 2

– No me permitáis todo. Ya sé que no lo puedo tener todo, pero os voy a poner a prueba.
No temáis ser firmes conmigo. Prefiero que me pongáis normas, porque así me siento segura.
No dejéis que coja malas costumbres. Cuento con vosotros para detectarlas y evitarlas.
No me hagáis sentir pequeña. Me hace querer actuar como si fuera grande y tonta.
No me corrijáis delante de extraños. Presto más atención si lo hacéis cuando estamos solos.
No me hagáis sentir que mis errores son pecados. Altera mis valores.
No me protejáis de las consecuencias de mis acciones. A veces tengo que aprender sufriéndolas.
No me regañéis ni me aconsejéis demasiado. Me tendré que proteger fingiendo ser sorda.

---

3 Students pretend they are an infant and write a letter to a parent explaining what he or she would need for a bright future in life.

4 Students read the text and answer the questions in their own words.

5 Students study the advertisement and answer the questions orally.

6 Students listen to the recording and answer the questions in English.

P 121, actividad 6

¿El turismo es siempre enemigo del medio ambiente? Pues no, cuando permite a la vez que los visitantes aprecien la naturaleza y que la población local la pueda explotar sin tener que destrozarla. Si el medio ambiente es lo que les proporciona el trabajo, los trabajadores querrán protegerlo.
En Costa Rica está el hotel Punta Islita, único en el mundo. El interés de los turistas hace que el hotel pueda contar con un equipo de biólogos que estudian y protegen las especies en peligro de extinción, como las tortugas que van a la zona a poner sus huevos o las aves tropicales.
No creas que tienes que ser hippie para disfrutarlo: es un hotel de lujo, con un spa completísimo, suites y mini-villas, todo construido con materiales naturales al estilo autóctono.

Answers:

Answers should contain:

1 *When tourists don't abuse it.*

2 *It is for biologists who want to study rare species.*

3 *turtles and birds* 4 *It is a luxury hotel.*

5 *It is built out of natural local materials.*

Unidad 9 Estudios y trabajo

Unit objectives

By the end of this unit students will be able to:

♦ Discuss their experiences of primary and secondary school
♦ Compare aspects of the education systems in Spain, Mexico and the UK
♦ Talk and write about study skills and strategies
♦ Consider employment options and how the world of work is changing

Grammar

By the end of this unit students will be able to:

♦ Use time clauses correctly
♦ Use commands correctly
♦ Use the subjunctive to express purpose
♦ Use all types of pronouns
♦ Use the subjunctive in relative clauses

Skills:

By the end of this unit students will be able to:

♦ Work out meaning without using a dictionary
♦ Write formal letters

Resources

♦ Students' Book pages 122 and 123
♦ CD 3, track 2

1a Group discussion. Students discuss their experiences of primary school and their memories of the aspects mentioned.

1b Students share their best and worst memory of their secondary education with the rest of the group. They should be encouraged to justify their opinions.

 2 Students listen to the four speakers and decide whether statements 1–10 are correct, incorrect or it isn't known.

P 122, actividad 2

– Me llamo Susana y recuerdo que me encantaba el colegio primario porque siempre podíamos jugar y estar libres del estrés de los exámenes. Tenía pocas amigas pero no me importaba porque jugaba y me divertía con ellas.
– Yo me llamo Carlos y recuerdo que me sentía siempre solo en la escuela primaria. Por eso me gustó más la secundaria porque allí tenía muchos amigos. Nos interesaban bastante las clases de inglés y francés pero lo que era en física o en química era nulo. Después de las clases siempre íbamos al polideportivo a pasar toda la tarde jugando al baloncesto.

– Soy Pedro y os cuento que mis recuerdos son algo vagos porque odiaba ir al cole. Siempre quería hacer música y ahora vivo de eso. Nunca tuve mucha dificultad en el colegio con las materias y aprobé los exámenes sin problema aunque estudiaba poco.
– Aquí voy yo – Fabiola – y os cuento que aunque no fui ningún genio siempre aprobé todos los exámenes y saqué buenas notas. Ahora que estoy trabajando estoy muy contenta de haber estudiado una carrera interesante y de tener un buen futuro.

Answers:
1 *se equivoca* **2** *no se sabe* **3** *se equivoca*
4 *tiene razón* **5** *tiene razón* **6** *no se sabe*
7 *no se sabe* **8** *se equivoca*

3a Students familiarise themselves with the given plan of subjects taught throughout the Spanish education system.

3b Students compare the British and Spanish education systems and make a list of similarities and differences, building sentences using the key phrases. Be sure to bring the main difference to their attention, which is that the A level equivalent is the *Bachillerato*, where one has to study substantially more subjects. Access to university not only depends on this (50%), but also on the results of the national exams called *La Selectividad* (50%).

4a Explain to students that to gain access to certain degree studies, students must follow the correct route and have achieved the required level in the required optional subjects. For example, to qualify to study medicine one would need to have completed Option A during E.S.O, and then the Health Option with all possible science options.

Students then look at the professions and decide which route they think the professionals would have followed.

4b Students reflect on their future plans and explain what options they would choose if they lived in Spain.

Educación para todos

Grammar focus

♦ Time clauses

Skills focus

♦ How to work out meaning without using a dictionary

Resources

♦ Students' Book pages 124 and 125

♦ CD 3, track 3

♦ Hoja 43

1a Students read the article for gist, and following the given example, they write just one sentence for each paragraph explaining what it is about. Some ideas would be:

Para 2: two principles of Telesecundaria

Para 3: how it works

Para 4: evaluation

Para 5: disadvantages and future

1b Students read the article a second time, this time aiming to get more detailed information. They then answer the questions 1–5.

Answers:

1 un sistema de educación basado en el uso de la televisión

2 más de 30 años

3 seis (repetidos mañana/tarde)

4 porque ha dado acceso a la educación a estudiantes de comunidades aisladas. Ellos terminan su educación con niveles comparables a otros estudiantes.

5 problemas technológicas y horarios estrictos

1c Students use the work on the two previous activities to write a short summary that captures the main points of the article.

Técnica

How to avoid using a dictionary.

A

1 acercar

2 afrontar, conllevar, abarcar

B

1 primer

2 isla

 2a Students listen to the radio programme and decide whether statements 1–5 are true or false.

P 125, actividad 2a

– El 19 de mayo, la Secretaria de Educación nos contaba que, para celebrar el 23 aniversario de la creación del subsistema telesecundaria del estado de Michoacán, se organizarán diversas actividades dirigidas a la promoción y difusión de las tareas que realiza este sistema educativo. La telesecundaria está presente en 803 escuelas de los municipios del estado, donde trabajan 2.740 profesores. Según nos decía el jefe del Departamento de Telesecundaria,

actualmente las 2.291 aulas acogen a 53.318 alumnos.

– Durante su visita, la secretaria nos informó de que los días 23 y 24 de mayo se llevará a cabo el Primer Coloquio de Adolescentes de Telesecundaria, que tiene como objetivo facilitar un espacio de debate para la reflexión en torno a la situación académica, social y educativa de los jóvenes.

– Durante las jornadas, se instalarán diez mesas de trabajo donde los 108 representantes de los municipios tocarán temas como: mitos y realidades de mi sexualidad adolescente, la familia y la escuela telesecundaria, las adicciones, mi proyecto de vida y autoestima, entre muchos otros.

Answers:

1 F 2 V 3 V 4 F 5 F

 2b Students listen again and answer the questions.

Answers:

1 23 aniversario de la creación de la Telesecundaria

2 Reflexionar sobre la situación académica, social y educativa de los jóvenes

3 Mitos y realidades de la sexualidad adolescente / la familia y la escuela telesecundaria / las adicciones / proyectos de vida / autoestima

3a Students reflect on the feasibility of the Telesecundaria in rural areas of the UK considering all the factors noted on the illustration. They write an essay of 200 words either supporting the idea or against it. Remind students to use the skills box on page 105.

3b Students use the essay written for activity 3a to help them prepare a 3-minute oral presentation of their argument, and be able to give answers to questions afterwards.

Gramática

Time clauses.

A 1 *... después de que haya concluido la retransmisión ... .* **2** *... antes de que empiece la nueva teleclase.*

B 1 *termine* **2** *estudio* **3** *llegara / llegase* **4** *encienda*

Asuntos de estudiantes

Grammar focus

♦ Commands

Key language

¡Empezad ...!

¡Haced ...!

¡Estudiad ...!
¡Intentad ...!
¡Aseguraos ...!
¡No dejéis ...!

Resources
- Students' Book pages 126 and 127
- CD 3, track 4
- Hojas 42, 43, 44
- Grammar Workbook page 60

1a Students match the four e-mails on the 'Problems' page (A–D) written to Maruja with her responses and advice (1–4).

Answers:
A *3*   **B** *2*   **C** *1*   **D** *4*

1b Students write an imaginary response to Federico's e-mail, using the imperative.

Gramática

Commands.

Answers:
A *2, 3, 4*

B **1** *¡No hagas payasadas!* **2** *¡Deja al perro en paz!* **3** *¡No te encierres en el baño!* **4** *¡Ven aquí inmediatamente!* **5** *¡Baja el volumen de la tele!* **6** *¡Acaba tus deberes!*

C **1** *¡Guardad / guarden silencio!* **2** *¡No utilicéis / utilicen los teléfonos móviles!* **3** *¡No copiéis / copien!* **4** *¡Permaneced sentados! / ¡Permanezcan sentados!*

2 Pair work. Ask students to think up another problem a young person might have, and in turns, they give their verbal advice on the problem to a partner, who must try to guess, from the advice given, what the imaginary problem is. This could also be done as a group activity / game where all students write an imaginary problem on a post-it. All post-its are collected and redistributed making sure none of the students gets the problem they wrote. Place a post-it on each student's forehead without their having seen the problem. They must then go around the class asking for advice from others until they guess what the problem being aired is.

3a First, students read the 12 pieces of advice in the "Little Book of Calm" panel.

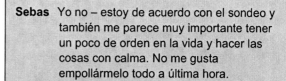

3b Then students listen to the recording and decide which of the pieces of advice are mentioned by Ana and Sebas.

P 127, actividad 3b
Ana   Voy a rellenar este sondeo sobre los estudios. Ay, caramba, siempre dicen lo mismo que hay que empezar desde ahora – cuando yo prefiero dejarlo todo para mañana.

Sebas   Yo no – estoy de acuerdo con el sondeo y también me parece muy importante tener un poco de orden en la vida y hacer las cosas con calma. No me gusta empollármelo todo a última hora.

Ana   Pues, vale, pero eso de comenzar por la mañana me parece obvio, ¿no?

Sebas   No siempre – yo trabajo mejor por la noche. Pero eso de escribir un plan es buena idea con tal de que no pases todo el tiempo escribiéndolo y no hagas las tareas.

Ana   Sí, de acuerdo. Hay muchas personas que se pasan la vida con listas y planes pero no logran terminar nada. Mis padres dicen que debo estudiar cuatro horas cada noche como mínimo.

Sebas   Uf no, eso es mucho – debes hacer dos o tres horas como máximo y siempre dicen que debes estar en un lugar tranquilo – pero yo puedo estudiar con la tele o con la radio puesta con el volumen bajo.

Ana   Yo también – incluso tengo que tener algo de ruido; si no me siento intranquila y me gusta estudiar acompañada y hablar con mis amigos.

Sebas   Sí, es bueno compartir las ideas y hablar o mandar emails o mensajes.

Ana   A mí los deberes y los exámenes nunca me han preocupado mucho – soy una persona muy tranquila en cuanto a los estudios.

Sebas   Ya lo creo – pero yo tengo que pasar el año. No quiero suspender ni una materia y por eso me parece una tontería decir que no importa catear – a mí sí me importa.

Answers:
Ana: 1, 4, 6, 10, 11
Sebas: 3, 5, 7

4 Using the command form, students design a poster for their fellow students, giving advice on how to study. They are asked to draw on the key phrases, but they should be encouraged to also use others of their own.

5 Pair work. Students toss a coin to see whether they should support or rebuke each of the statements in the seven boxes. You could set a time limit and explain that they have to speak for 1 or 2 minutes to present their view before the argument / debate starts.

Un panorama laboral incierto

Grammar focus
- The subjunctive to express purpose

Key language

Es importante que ...
Debería ser ...
Lo crucial es ...
Es de suma importancia que sepa ...
Es imperativo que tenga ...

Resources

♦ Students' Book pages 128 and 129
♦ CD 3, track 5

1 Students look at the illustration and answer the questions.

2a Students read the article and answer the questions.

Answers:

1 *310.000*

2 pocas oportunidades laborales para gente de esa edad / terminaron su educación en una década con alta tasa de desempleo

3 los jóvenes / porque no tienen experiencia y por eso tienen dificultad en encontrar un trabajo convencional

4 el desarrollo y abaratamiento de las TICs

5 para no perder empleados clave y poder reclutar nuevos trabajadores de alto calibre

6 el telempleo va a crecer e incluso va a tener un carácter más internacional

2b Students practise their translating skills by translating the highlighted paragraphs.

2c Writing exercise. Students write their opinion in 150 words, justifying their answer with examples. Encourage students to give and justify their opinion relating to the social changes that affect the work environment and expectations in their own country.

3 Students list the personal characteristics that they feel are needed to be a successful *teletrabajador*. In doing so they use the key phrases.

Gramática

The subjunctive to express purpose.

Answers:

A warning, requesting, advising, with value judgements, with doubt and probability and with possibility and impossibility

B *Claro está que para que el trabajo a distancia <u>sea</u> posible, se han debido desarrollar y perfeccionar las TICs.* Clearly ICTs has had to be developed and perfected to make distance working possible.

Así como abaratar el coste de los equipos y del software que ahora permite que muchos <u>habiliten</u> un espacio laboral en su domicilio a un precio asequible.

Such as bringing down the cost of equipment and software which now allows that many (people) organise a work space at home at a reasonable price.

C 1 *cuide* **2** *encontrara* **3** *llegué*
  4 *practique* **5** *busca*

4a Students listen to some answers to an interview and work out which question the interviewee was answering in each case.

P 129, actividad 4

– Hoy nos acompaña Don Miguel Soto del Oso, directivo de una de las firmas de selección de personal con mejor reputación del país. Buenas tardes, Don Miguel, es un placer tenerle con nosotros.

– Buenas tardes, el placer es mío.

– Don Miguel, ¿cuáles son las cualidades del trabajador ideal de nuestra época?

– A ver… recientemente hemos hecho un estudio para definir el perfil del profesional ideal y los resultados demuestran que además de una buena formación y conocimientos de idiomas, hay otros cinco atributos que son los más buscados: disponibilidad para la movilidad geográfica; creatividad, innovación e imaginación; multiculturalidad; flexibilidad, y orientación hacia resultados.

– ¿Parece que la formación y la experiencia pierden importancia, no?

– Todavía son deseables, pero todo está cambiando y las características personales y la capacidad de adaptación y de tomar las riendas del propio desarrollo son cada vez más importantes.

– Hablemos de la movilidad geográfica. ¿Por qué es tan importante?

– Bueno, a veces los mejores profesionales no viven donde se les necesita. Por ejemplo, en nuestra empresa, la búsqueda de profesionales en otros países además de España es una práctica habitual.

– Ya veo. ¿Cómo se compara esta situación con la de hace unos años?

– Para que vea, hace sólo dos años, el 95% se cubría tras una búsqueda en el país donde se ofertaba el empleo. Entonces era algo impensable, y a una empresa cliente no se le podía decir que venía un candidato extranjero. Ahora, por el contrario, las multinacionales valoran que sus profesionales sean capaces de trabajar en una filial de cualquier país del mundo.

– La segunda de las virtudes identificadas, la innovación o creatividad …

– Sí, está relacionada con la competitividad. Hoy en día hacer las cosas mejor no basta, sino que, además, hay que hacerlas de otro modo, de forma más innovadora e imaginativa que el resto.

– Nos comentaba que otro atributo es la multiculturalidad. ¿Se refiere a los idiomas?
– No, no sólo a los idiomas. La multiculturalidad va más allá: significa haber trabajado en otros países o en empresas donde no todos los empleados son del mismo lugar. Así, la mente se abre, y uno se adapta a los cambios más fácilmente.
– Por último, ¿a qué se refiere cuando menciona la orientación hacia resultados?
– Bueno, al final los resultados se traducen en dinero, así que el profesional ideal debe tener una capacidad extraordinaria para alcanzar las metas y los objetivos marcados por su empresa.
– Debemos dejarlo aquí. Muchas gracias, Don Miguel.
Y ahora el turno para nuestros oyentes. Y tú, ¿qué piensas? Llámanos al 91 869 9234 ...

4b Students listen to the whole interview and check that their answers to 4a are correct.

Answers:

A *4* **B** *5* **C** *1* **D** *3* **E** *2*

4c Students listen again to the interview if needed and choose the words from the grid that complete the sentences in the paragraph. Point out that each word can only be used once, and that there are some words that will be left over.

Answers:

a *unas características* **b** *aumentado* **c** *la sucursal*
d *la habilidad* **e** *la multiculturalidad* **f** *trabajado*
g *flexibilidad* **h** *alcance*

5 Students prepare a 3-minute presentation in which they sell themselves as the ideal professional that Don Miguel would want to employ. They should be encouraged to illustrate their arguments with examples.

La búsqueda del trabajo

Grammar focus
♦ Pronouns
♦ The subjunctive in relative clauses

Skills focus
♦ Writing formal letters

Resources
♦ Students' Book pages 130–131
♦ CD 3, track 7
♦ Hojas 41, 45
♦ Grammar Workbook pages 22, 57

1a Students read the article and decide if the statements 1–6 agree, disagree or are not mentioned.

Answers:

1 *no se menciona* **2** *contradice – sólo para jóvenes*

3 *está de acuerdo* **4** *contradice – ayuda a todos los jóvenes / no hay requisitos*
5 *está de acuerdo* **6** *no se menciona*

1b Students write a short summary (50 to 75 words) of the article capturing the main points.

Gramática

Pronouns.

Answers:

A 1 *Ellos buscan trabajo.* **2** *Le prometí que iría a la entrevista.* **3** *Tina lo escribe.*
4 *Hablé con la Srta Pérez quien me ayudó.*

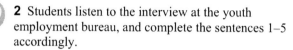

2 Students listen to the interview at the youth employment bureau, and complete the sentences 1–5 accordingly.

P 130, actividad 2

– Nos gustaría saber más sobre los idiomas que habla ... ¿Cuántos idiomas habla usted?
– Hablo tres idiomas: inglés, francés y español por supuesto – bueno, cuatro con el catalán.
– ¿Cuánto tiempo hace que estudia francés?
– Lo estudio desde hace cinco años.
– ¿Sigue estudiando inglés?
– Pues sí, sigo estudiando por las noches porque me interesa sobre todo mantener mi nivel oral.
– Dice aquí que lleva apenas dos meses en su empleo actual. ¿Por qué quiere dejarlo?
– La verdad es que no es el tipo de empleo que busco pero lo cogí porque necesitaba dinero.
– ¿Hacía cuánto tiempo que estudiaba en el colegio cuando empezó a estudiar inglés?
– Llevaba dos años porque empezamos los cursos de inglés cuando tenía 8 años.
– ¿Por qué cree usted que es importante hablar varios idiomas?
– Pues, porque es imprescindible si uno quiere trabajar en un departamento de ventas o en el extranjero.
– ¿Qué ventajas cree usted que tiene hablar varios idiomas a la hora de conseguir un empleo?
– Bueno, siempre hay más oportunidades si hablas un idioma tanto en el tipo de empleo que consigues como en la promoción interna, creo.

Suggested answers:
1 *... su nivel oral* **2** *... necesitaba dinero*
3 *... los ocho años* **4** *... trabajar en ventas o viajar*
5 *... más oportunidades laborales*

3 Students debate whether they agree or disagree with the statement.

Gramática

The subjunctive in relative clauses.

Answers:

A **1** *Busco a un empleado que sea perfecto.*

2 *Necesito a la secretaria que habla español.*

3 *No encuentro ningún trabajo que sea adecuado.*

4 *Es posible que no exista.*

4a Students read the letter in the next column and seek out the alternative words or phrases for those listed.

Answers:

1 *en respuesta a* **2** *un cordial saludo* **3** *el puesto de*
4 *les agradezco* **5** *que adjunto (adjuntar)*
6 *campo* **7** *quedo a su disposición*
8 *Estimados señores* **9** *dato* **10** *que requieren*

4b Students translate the letter maintaining the same level of formality and business tone.

Técnica

Writing formal letters.

A Students write a job application letter. You may wish to extend the number of vacancies for which they can apply or get the students to do some research themselves and find a suitable position that they would be interested in.

Gramática en acción

Resources

♦ Students' Book page 132

A

Answers:

1 *que* **2** *los cuales* **3** *donde* **4** *que* **5** *Quienes*
6 *el cual* **7** *cuyo* **8** *que*

B

Answers:

1 *Las tres salas de reuniones que se necesitan, se encuentran en la planta baja.*

2 *Recepción, donde hay té, café, y refrescos, está cerca de la entrada.*

3 *Sara es la secretaria cuyas labores son extraordinarias.*

4 *El programa Proniño, que promueve la escolarización en Latinoamérica, es muy popular.*

C

Examples:

Me gustaría pertenecer a una organización cuyo objetivo sea caritativo y sin ánimo de lucro.

Me gustaría tener unas vacaciones que duren seis semanas.

Quisiera tener un jefe que trate a sus empleados de una forma justa.

A escoger

Resources

♦ Students' Book page 133
♦ CD 3, track 8

1a Students list the advantages and disadvantages of wearing a school uniform.

1b Students listen to the speaker and choose the correct option in each case.

> **P 133, actividades 1b**
>
> ¿Uniforme o ropa casual? ¡Uniforme mil veces! Así todos vamos iguales y nos evitamos la molestia de escoger nuestra ropa cada mañana. Además, me molesta desperdiciar mi ropa en lucirla en la escuela, prefiero el uniforme que, aunque no nos guste, debemos admitir que evita problemas de discriminación y las envidias y críticas de mal gusto. Si vas al colegio con tu propia ropa, después no sabes ni que ponerte cuando vas a salir, porque no puedes llevar lo que ya has llevado al colegio. Claro, estoy de acuerdo con los que dicen que con tu ropa te puedes expresar mejor y estar más cómoda contigo misma y resaltar tus encantos y todo eso, pero... ¿te imaginas toda la ropa que tendrías que tener para ir al colegio con algo diferente cada día? ¡Cuánto gasto! Sería muchísimo. El uniforme crea un sentimiento de pertenencia e identidad hacia una institución y eso es bueno. Además, si tu colegio tiene uniforme, lo interesante es que te ves diferente cuando sales con tus amigos fuera del colegio.

Answers:

1 *b* **2** *b* **3** *b*

1c Students listen again and choose the order in which a–f are mentioned by the young woman.

Answers:

f, b, d, a, e, c

2 Students read the opinions that explain the practice and consequences of re-sits and repeating a year in the same class. They work with a partner to list the advantages. They then compare these advantages to the advantages of their own educational system.

Cultural note: In Spain it is regular practice to assess all students at the end of every school year from Primary level. If students achieve less than 50 per cent in a subject, they fail the subject and have to re-sit exams at the beginning of September before regular school starts. Students can only carry forward two failed subjects. Therefore if, after September re-sits, they still have less than 50 per cent in more than two subjects, they would be required to repeat the year. This causes a situation whereby a student could turn 16 and yet be in Year 2 of E.S.O. (equivalent to UK Year 9) and so on. There is an on-going debate about this practice between supporters and those that disagree. However, despite the several educational reforms that have taken place in the last decade, this issue has still not been addressed.

3 Students write an essay about the practice of repeating a year in the same class in Spain, highlighting and justifying both its advantages and disadvantages. They should also present their own opinions.

Técnica

Students remind themselves of the importance of checking their work, and aspects to look out for.

Repaso Unidad 9

Resources

- Students' Book pages 134–135
- CD 3, tracks 9–11

1a Students listen carefully for the three details relating to each of the students.

P 134, actividad 1a

- Bueno, bienvenidos a todos. En la clase de hoy vamos a hablar sobre vuestro progreso en los estudios. Primero quiero que me digáis en qué asignaturas vais bien y en cuáles vais mal. Luego quiero que me indiquéis la optativa que habéis escogido y quiero que me expliquéis por qué la habéis elegido. **Luis**, vamos a comenzar contigo.
- Pues, profe, yo creo que voy muy bien en historia y geo – siempre me han gustado estas materias. Tengo ciertos problemas con la economía – es la parte de las matemáticas que me parece algo difícil, pero no es nada grave. He escogido humanidades porque me parecen muy útiles para seguir una carrera más tarde.
- Y a ti, **Alicia** – ¿cómo te va?
- Bien, bien en todas las materias comunes y en dibujo artístico pero no me va muy bien en dibujo técnico – a decir verdad me va bastante mal. He elegido la modalidad de artes plásticas porque siempre me ha encantado dibujar pero libremente – nada de eso de técnica – esto no me llama la atención. He elegido esta opción porque voy a seguir estudiando todas las formas de las artes y luego quiero ser diseñadora de ropa en Zara.
- ¡Qué lástima! A ver, **Jairo**, ¿cómo te va?
- A mí me va bien en las materias comunes pero no estoy muy seguro de las materias de química y biología – son más difíciles de lo que había

---

pensado. Creo que me va más o menos bien y me gusta la optativa de economía. Estoy cursando Ciencias de la Naturaleza y de la Salud porque quiero ser enfermero.
- **Elena**, ¿tú qué me cuentas?
- Ay, profe, no tengo mucha esperanza – creo que me he equivocado al elegir tecnología.
- Quería estudiar informática nada más pero aquí en el cole me han puesto a estudiar matemáticas y física también y no sirvo para esto. Creo que será mejor cambiar a formación profesional media donde puedo seguir la carrera que me gusta más – la de diseñadora de páginas web.
- **Ramón**, a ti te va bien, espero.
- Sí, señorita – A mí me va bien en todo porque me había informado bastante bien antes de elegir la modalidad de ciencias. Me encantan las matemáticas y ahora he sacado buenas notas en física también, así que no voy mal en nada. La tecnología me va a servir de mucho en el futuro, de eso estoy seguro.

Answers:

Luis: *geografía e historia* ✓, *economía* ✗.
Ha escogido humanidades porque le servirán en su carrera.
Alicia: *materias comunes y dibujo artístico* ✓, *dibujo técnico* ✗.
Ha elegido la modalidad de artes plásticas porque quiere ser diseñadora con la casa Zara.
Jairo: *informática* ✓, *química y biología* ✗, *economía* ✓. *Ha escogido ciencias porque quiere ser enfermero.*
Elena: *informática* ✓, *matemáticas y física* ✗.
Ha escogido tecnología porque quiere ser diseñadora de páginas web.
Ramón: *matemáticas y física* ✓. *Ha escogido la tecnología porque le servirá en el futuro.*

1b Students listen again for details about Luis and note the differences.

Possible answers:

Luis cree	El profe dice…
Va bien en historia	Tiene dificultades en historia
Tiene problemas en economía	Está progresando en economía
No va bien en matemáticas	Entiende bien las matemáticas

2a Students read Miguel's passage and decide if the statements are true, false or are not mentioned. As an extension activity you could ask students to rephrase the statements that are untrue.

Answers:

1 *F*	2 *no se sabe*	3 *V*	4 *V*	5 *F*
6 *F*	7 *no se sabe*	8 *V*		

2b Students listen to Paulina's passage and answer the questions.

Answers:

1 *Alguien que trabaja con la madera y/o diseña o construye muebles.*

2 *Es una persona práctica y sociable.*

3 *No, está cursando Formación Profesional.*

4 *Cuando apruebe el curso porque hay más oportunidades allí.*

5 *Porque tiene tres hermanos más que quieren estudiar y no habrá suficiente dinero para pagar sus estudios.*

P 135, actividad 2b

Pues, a mí me gustaría ser ebanista porque me encanta trabajar con la madera. Me entusiasma el diseño y me encanta tratar con la gente – soy bastante sociable. Estoy cursando Formación Profesional de grado medio en tecnología de la informática porque soy una persona práctica. Si apruebo el curso iré a la capital donde hay más oportunidades de encontrar empleo como ebanista. Tendré que ganar lo suficiente para mantenerme porque tengo tres hermanos más que tienen la intención de seguir estudiando. Ellos tendrán que seguir viviendo en casa si quieren ir a la universidad, ¡porque no habrá manera de pagar sus estudios!

2c Students use Luís and Paulina's passages as examples to write one of their own talking about their own aspirations and future intentions.

3a Students listen for detail and check which of the worries is mentioned.

P 135, actividad 3a

A No sé por dónde empezar a buscar un empleo.
B No hay trabajos permanentes.
C Tengo tantos títulos que nadie me querrá emplear.
D No hemos recibido ninguna orientación en el colegio.
E No tengo la menor idea de lo que quiero hacer.
F Aquí en España hay muchos médicos sin trabajo.
G Mis padres me dicen que es una profesión de mujeres.
H Los hombres siempre tienen sueldos más altos.
I Hay demasiadas mujeres en enfermería.
J Para mí la única forma de conseguir un puesto es a través de las oposiciones.

Answers:

| A 7 | B 6 | C 5 | D 7 | E 7 |
| F 1 | G 2/3 | H 3 | I 2/3 | J 4 |

3b Students discuss which of the mentioned work issues worry them. They should be encouraged to talk about and illustrate their views with their own experiences or those of people they know. It is possible that you may be able to link this exercise to current affairs if any relevant piece reaches the news or if any related TV programmes are been shown (such as *The Apprentice*).

4a Students read the interview questions and classify them according to the topic they relate to.

Answers:

Formación 3, 7;   Pasado profesional 1, 4;
Motivo de la solicitud 8, 9;
Comportamiento en el trabajo 5, 12, 14;
Proyectos 10, 15;   Personalidad 2, 6, 11, 16, 17;
Retribución 13, 18

4b Students reorder the questions in a logical order and then interview a partner. It would be a good idea to let the students choose the position and company they are being interviewed for, and they should be given a little time to prepare answers. Students acting as interviewers should be encouraged to ask some additional questions according to the answers to add a surprise/unexpected element to the conversation.

Suggested order:
Motivo de la solicitud, formación, personalidad, pasado profesional, comportamiento en el trabajo, proyectos, retribución

5 Students write a formal letter to an employer (perhaps the same as used in activity 4b) showing an interest in being taken on for work experience. Students should ensure the correct level of formality and adequate language register are used, and they should refer to page 131 if necessary. Students must ensure that they briefly answer questions 3, 4, 8, 9, 10 and 16 of the interview guide in their letter.

Repaso final

Escuchar

Resources
- Students' Book page 136
- CD 3, tracks 12–15

 1a Students listen to the publicity campaign for gist and identify the message.

P 136, actividad 1a

– Cuando bebes, te crees el doble de fuerte, el doble de guapo, el doble de ligón, el doble de gracioso, pero en realidad eres el doble de ridículo. El alcohol daña tu cuerpo y a tu celebro, el alcohol te destroza por partida doble. Ministerio de Sanidad y Consumo.

– Cuando bebes, te crees el doble de simpática, el doble de guapa, el doble de graciosa, el doble de sexy, pero en realidad eres el doble de vulnerable. El alcohol daña tu cuerpo y tu cerebro, el alcohol te destroza por partida doble. Ministerio de Sanidad y Consumo.

Suggested answers:
El alcohol da a los jóvenes un sentimiento falso de autoestima.
El alcohol destruye tu vida.
El alcohol reduce el sentido común y el juicio de los jóvenes haciéndoles más ridículos / vulnerables.

 1b Students listen again and list the adjectives used in each track and then translate them.

Answers:
Boy: fuerte – *strong;* guapo – *handsome;*
  ligón – *flirty (more able to "pull");*
  gracioso – *funny;* ridículo – *ridiculous*
Girl: simpática – *bubbly;* guapa – *pretty;*
  graciosa – *funny;* sexy – *sexy;*
  vulnerable – *vulnerable*

 2a Students listen for gist and decide whether the speakers have a mobile phone dependency or not.

P 136, actividad 2a

1 Creo que tengo cierta dependencia ... a veces, cuando me he dejado el móvil en el coche o en casa, me siento como limitada, como vacía. Entonces me entra la paranoia y me preocupa que, si voy a llegar tarde a algún sitio o algo así, no puedo avisar.

2 ¿Que si dependo de él? ¡Para nada! Tengo móvil, pero si estoy en casa es raro que sepa dónde está sin llamarlo desde el fijo. Creo que

---

es muy buena solución para estar siempre disponible si alguien nos necesita, pero también es una especie de cárcel de la que no puedes escapar ni para ir al baño.

3 Bueno, en ocasiones es necesario para comunicar algo a ciertas personas. Diría que es más cómodo, pero no es para nada un elemento vital para mí; por lo menos yo resuelvo las cosas aunque me haya dejado el móvil en casa.

4 ¿Dependo de mi móvil ...? Uy, espera ... antes de contestarte déjame que lo busque que ya hace un rato que no lo veo.

5 Yo suelo pasar bastante del móvil. Hay días que lo cojo pero se me olvida encenderlo y lo llevo apagado todo el día. Lo tengo para usarlo en caso de necesidad o emergencia, pero por lo general, me agobia bastante que me molesten llamándome al móvil.

6 Hubo un tiempo en el que dependía mucho de él pero ahora ya no, con lo cual he llegado a la conclusión de que no hay nada que sea imprescindible.

7 No, de hecho siempre anda perdido por casa y solamente lo cojo cuando voy a salir del pueblo, por si se me avería el coche, para avisar a la grúa y cosas así. A decir verdad, más que otra cosa es un engorro eso de tener que llevarlo siempre encima.

8 Por desgracia sí, no lo puedo evitar... mi móvil es como mi maquillaje, si salgo sin él me siento desnuda. Además, mi jefe me llama continuamente y si no contesto... ¡No veas cómo se pone!

Answers:
dependent: 1, 4, 8; not dependent: 2, 3, 5, 6, 7

 2b Students listen again, this time for detail, and choose the statements mentioned or implied by each of the young people. Some of the statements may be used more than once.

Answers:

a *2*	b *2, 7*	c *1, 3, 5, 7*	d *8*	e *1, 4*
f *5*	g *2, 5*	h *2*		

 3a Students listen to the report and decide if the statements are true, untrue or not mentioned. You may wish to encourage students to correct false statements as an extension activity.

P 136, actividad 3a

El estudio reciente de un centro de orientación de Madrid concluye que cada vez menos jóvenes siguen su vocación y ahora se inclinan por ciclos formativos más cortos y con más salidas profesionales para poder ponerse a trabajar antes. Parece ser que las razones más

---

populares de este cambio son las elevadas notas necesarias para acceder a algunas carreras universitarias y la dificultad de estos estudios.

Las preferencias de los jóvenes han cambiado y, mientras hace una década solamente aparecían cinco ciclos de formación entre los veinte estudios más demandados, el año pasado ya eran diez los ciclos elegidos por los estudiantes. Carreras como Medicina, Educación y Psicología se mantienen todavía entre los primeros puestos aunque ya han sido superadas por la Formación Profesional de Administración y la de Mantenimiento de vehículos.

Los estudios profesionales para entrar en el cuerpo de Policía o de Bomberos sustituyen a los estudios militares que, habiendo ocupado la segunda posición en 1996, ahora sufren el descenso más destacado.

El centro de orientación también ha identificado la elección de estudios más común según el sexo de los estudiantes y ha concluido que las chicas se inclinan más por las carreras universitarias tales como Magisterio, Psicología y Medicina y por los ciclos de Imagen personal y Administración. Sin embargo, los chicos prefieren la formación profesional más técnica, como los ciclos de Mantenimiento de vehículos, Electrónica e Informática.

Answers:

1 *F*   **2** *V*   **3** *F*   **4** *V*   **5** *NSM*

3b Students listen to the report again and choose the adequate ending to each sentence according to what they hear.

Answers:

1 *b*   **2** *a*   **3** *b*   **4** *b*   **5** *b*   **6** *a*

3c Students listen once again if needed and answer the questions in English.

Answers:

1 *An increasing number of students choose not to follow their vocation and settle for formative courses (professional qualifications) because they are shorter and lead to an earlier working life. Also grades to gain access to university restrict entry and the degrees are more difficult.*

2 *They have become more popular than Medicine, Education and Psycology – the three most popular degrees.*

3 *Military studies used to occupy the second position for most popular study.*

4 *Girls prefer Teaching, Psycology and Medicine.*

5 *They prefer professional qualifications such as Vehicle Maintenance, Electronics and ICT.*

Hablar

Resources

♦ Students' Book page 137

1 As a whole class activity, or in small groups, students brainstorm the topics that cause friction between parents and teenage children and they explain the reasons why they cause problems in each case.

2a Students look at the poster and prepare a presentation as directed.

Cultural background: The campaign was directed at parents with teenagers or young people living at home. The problem it refers to is not so much that of alcohol abuse (as some students may propose), but the fact that parents often are unaware of what goes on in their household and how much their children really drink. Also, a problem of communication between parents and their children is implied. The objective of the campaign is to prevent teenage alcohol consumption, to inform the parents of the dangers and consequences of the alcohol consumption of their teenage children, and to foment communication to prevent the problem before it arises.

2b Role play: Students should be grouped in pairs, or groups of three, to represent the types of arguments likely to happen in Spanish households when teenage children don't get up until late afternoon following a night of drinking and arriving home late. Students should be encouraged to use the imperative.

3 Role play: Students play the part of a travel agent who has been charged with promoting the holiday type in the leaflet provided in the Student's Book.

You may choose to play the role of the Puerto Rican family, or perhaps choose to provide the information below to some of the students in your class so that they can complete the activity in pairs or small groups.

♦ There are four people in the family but they are not sure what type of holiday they are looking for because mum and the kids are very active but dad is unwell and he is unable to do strenuous exercise.

♦ There are two teenagers travelling, aged 14 and 17. The family will be travelling through other parts of Europe before arriving in Spain so they are flexible with regards to dates.

♦ They need to keep accommodation costs as low as possible so that they have sufficient money to spend on other activities.

♦ They have visited Malaga before, but they found it too touristy.

The student(s) taking the role of the travel agent must find out:

1 How many people are travelling, and the ages of any children.

2 How they intend to travel to Spain.

3 Have they visited Spain before?

4 What kind of holiday are they looking for?

5 What is their budget?

Then he / she must provide detailed information according to their needs.

Suggested information that should be mentioned:
The beauty of the surroundings
Location
'Paradores' – a good alternative
Different kinds of accommodation offers catering for all tastes and budgets: from 30 euros a night, breakfast included
Special offers during the low season
Variety on offer: art, nature, cuisine, culture, tradition, history and beauty
For the most adventurous: snorkelling, quads, karting, yachting, rafting, pot-holing, absailing, sailing schools and lots more
Possible ways of arriving in Galicia

To conclude, the student / travel agent should explain and justify why Galicia is a good choice. If students are not forthcoming, perhaps the family should directly ask if he / she has visited the area so that the student can improvise with an adequate answer.

Leer

Resources
♦ Students' Book pages 138–139

1a Students read the article for gist and decide what it is about.

Suggested answers:
Se trata de los problemas entre padres e hijos los fines de semana.
Se trata de la discordancia de opiniones relacionadas con el salir de los hijos los fines de semana.
Se trata de padres sobre-protectores, y sus preocupaciones de los fines de semana.

1b Students think of an adequate title for the article.

Suggested answer:
Fines de semana con adolescentes

1c Students scan the text and use the context to find a synonym of the listed words or phrases.

Answers:
1 *a causa*
2 *estar en vela*
3 *dormir de un tirón*
4 *receta*

1d Students now find antonyms for the words listed.

Answers:
1 *denso*
2 *confiar*
3 *peligrosa*
4 *cariño*

2 Translation exercise. Students translate the article, paying particular attention to maintaining the same language register.

Example translation:
On Friday evening the telephone lines are down and in the homes one can feel the tension. Disagreements start caused by problems with discussions about times to come home, making comparisons, and the other usual arguments. I am the only one who isn't allowed to come home at any time!
Spanish mothers stay awake until they hear their children arrive: I can't sleep properly until I hear the last one get home! For eight years I haven't slept at weekends!
We have to trust our children but nowadays being out at night is more dangerous: alcohol, drugs, accidents ...
Family breakfast no longer exists – Saturdays and Sundays – and sometimes even lunch is a problem. What is the solution? There is no recipe – but how about conversation, showing them affection and trust, and leading by example?

3 Students read the beginning part of the sentences and find a suitable ending to construct eight pieces of advice. You may wish to extend this activity by asking students if they agree or disagree with the resulting advice.

Answers:

1 *h*	2 *d*	3 *g*	4 *c*	5 *a*
6 *b*	7 *f*	8 *e*		

4a Students read the article and decide if the statements 1–8 are true, false or not mentioned. You may wish to extend the activity by asking students to correct the incorrect statements.

Cultural background: *¿Quién actúa esta noche?* was a drastic campaign used by the Spanish Ministry of Public Health during the summer of 2007. It was intended to raise the awareness of sexually transmitted diseases mainly arising as a result of summer flings among the young, who enjoy a three month summer holiday from schools, colleges and universities. Its effectiveness has yet to be analysed but it was intensely publicised as a series of 'cool' concert events, pitched to attract the attention of the young who were led to believe it was a genuine music campaign only to later realise with some shock that it was about the risks and ease with which an STD can be caught.

Answers:

1 *F* **2** *F* **3** *V* **4** *NSM* **5** *NSM*
6 *F* **7** *V* **8** *NSM*

5a Students choose the correct verb to fill in each of the gaps. They need to think about the context / meaning, the appropriate tense and the subject agreement.

Answers:

a *está causando* **b** *trata* **c** *preocupa* **d** *decide*
e *cuidar* **f** *consigue* **g** *tendrá* **h** *sobrevivir*
i *oculta* **j** *conocen* **k** *es* **l** *está basada*
m *ha tenido*

5b Students read the passage again to draw on key information. If students are familiar with the sitcom, you may choose to encourage further debate with regards to Betty's qualities and weaknesses.

Nombre: Betty / Bea

Edad: 26

Ocupación: secretaria de dirección

Cualidades: inteligente, bondadosa, bien preparada

Defectos: despreocupada por su aspecto físico

Escribir

Resources
♦ Students' Book page 140

The series of activities on this page are designed to practise all aspects of writing, including a variety of language registers and formal and informal writing.

For each of the activities students write the number of words indicated in the Students' Book, or by the teacher where appropriate.

Students should be reminded that they are required to:
♦ develop fully the topic,
♦ structure the work in a logical manner,
♦ use the appropriate language register,
♦ pay attention to the quality and variety of the language and grammar structures that they choose to use,
♦ express their opinion and justify it fully with facts, ideas, examples or proposals relevant to each occasion.

1a Students write their reaction to the news and give their opinion on the second question.

1b Students choose five people whom they idolise and explain why they admire them, fully justifying their choices.

2 Students write a passage about the three objects they would choose to take to a desert island, in the context of a virtual reality show. Students should be encouraged to have knowledge of similar shows in the UK to support and justify their own choices.

3 Students write a summary of the last episode of their favourite television sitcom or series. They should be reminded to use the passive voice where appropriate

4a Students choose their favourite current publicity campaign and answer the questions fully, ensuring that they provide factual information and examples as well as evidence to support their statements.

4b Students look at the poster on page 139 and answer the questions fully.

5 Students write a formal letter requesting the information listed.

6 Students read the question and argue their position in an essay.

Gramática

Resources
♦ Students' Book pages 141-143

Using *se* to avoid the passive voice

1 Students write a series of sentences in Spanish, using *se*.

Answers:
1 *Es posible que se exagere la importancia de la tecnología.*
2 *Aún no se han dejado de lado los medios de comunicación tradicionales.*
3 *Todavía no se han impuesto las nuevas tecnologías.*
4 *Se las va integrando de acuerdo a lo que realmente se necesita.*

Verbs with irregular forms in the preterite

2 Students complete the text with the correct forms of the verbs in the preterite.

Answers:
(le) *dije* *fue* *trajo* *puso* *quiso*
(lo) *vi* *tuvo* *pudo*

The future tense

3 Students rewrite the sentences using verbs in the future.

Answers:

1 *Iré un año a estudiar a Francia.*

2 *Podré aprender francés.*

3 *Esperaré salir de excursión los fines de semana a conocer el país./Saldré de excursión los fines de semana a conocer el país.*

4 *Mi hermano tendrá que quedarse en España.*

5 *Mi madre me echará de menos.*

6 *Nos veremos en las vacaciones de Navidad.*

Verbs with prepositions or followed by the infinitive

4a Students complete the sentences with the correct word from the choices given.

Answers:

1 *de*

2 *con*

3 *a*

4 *de*

5 *En*

6 *a   de*

Por or para?

4b Students decide whether *por* or *para* should be used in the sentences given.

Answers:

1 *para*

2 *para*

3 *por*

4 *para*

5 *por*

6 *para*

7 *Para*

8 *para*

The perfect tense

5a Students write sentences using the verb in the perfect tense.

Answers:

Han vendido la casa.

Han abierto el libro.

Se ha roto el brazo.

5b Students change the preterite tense verbs to the perfect.

Answers:

Hoy me he hecho rica. He descubierto que he ganado la lotería. Le he dicho a mi jefe que ya no quiero trabajar allí y he escrito a mi novio para decirle adiós. Me he ido de casa y no he vuelto.

Pronouns

6a Students translate the sentences given into Spanish using the correct pronouns.

Answers:

1 *Fue con <u>ella</u> a ver una película.*

2 *<u>Ella</u> ya la había visto.*

3 *Ella <u>le</u> dijo <u>lo</u> que pasaba al final.*

4 *Él ya no <u>la</u> va a volver a invitar.*

6b Students choose the appropriate words to complete the text.

Answers:

1 *mí*

2 *lo*

3 *nos*

4 *se*

5 *cuya*

The subjunctive

7 Students identify which verbs are in the infinitive.

Answers:

1 *quiera*

2 *digan*

3 *comáis*

4 *pongas*

5 *viva*

6 *deje*

7 *jueguen*

8 Students decide whether the subjunctive is needed or not in the sentences given, and write the sentences in Spanish.

Answers:

1 *Quiere ir a esquiar.*

2 *Te aconseja que dejes de fumar.*

3 *Pienso que la tecnología es una pérdida de tiempo.*

4 *Tengo la impresión de que no va a funcionar.*

5 *Resulta imposible que los padres controlen a sus hijos./A los padres les resulta imposible controlar a sus hijos.*

6 *Es una pena que no estés de acuerdo conmigo.*

9 Students use the subjunctive when writing the beginning of an answer to the questions given.

Answers:

2 *No me parece que sea importante comprar siempre el último modelo porque…*

3 *Te recomiendo que escuches diferentes tipos de música y luego…*

4 *No creo que debas preguntarme a mí porque…*

5 *No es tan difícil pensar que el gobierno pueda…*

10 Students complete the table with verbs from the text below.

Answers:

Presente	Perfecto	Pretérito	Imperfecto	Otros
tiene	ha convertido	descubrió	mascaban	buscando
		fue	extraía	haciendo
		extendieron	estaba	mejorar
				fabricar
				vender
				consumir

11 Students choose the correct word to complete the text.

Answers:

1 *por*

2 *él*

3 *que*

4 *ver lo*

5 *tú*

6 *sirva*

7 *atrajo*

8 *de*

12 Students complete the sentences adapting the phrases that are underlined in the text.

Answers:

2 *... conozcamos los mejores lugares.*

3 *... acudamos a la página web del ecoagroturismo.*

4 *... sido recogidos/se han recogido hasta 160 ejemplos de ecoturismo.*

5 *... hoteles y museos.*

6 *... está estudiando la manera de englobar todos esos lugares bajo una misma etiqueta.*

13 Students match the two sentence halves.

1 *e*

2 *d*

3 *b*

4 *g*

5 *f*

6 *c*

7 *a*

Técnica

Resources

♦ Students' Book pages 144-145

♦ CD 3, track 15

Dealing with statistics

1 Students look at the table of statistics and say which of the conclusions can be justified.

Answers:

1   2   3   4

Listening: taking notes

2a Students listen and take notes so that they can explain the general argument.

CD 3, track 15   P 144, actividades 2 y 3

El sondeo de los valores de los españoles ofrece una perspectiva interesante. A primera vista retrata un país preocupado por el sistema de salud. Pero al investigarlo por edades, nos damos cuenta de que el español "típico" con la escala de valores presentada en las conclusiones no existe en la realidad.

Si nos fijamos en los jóvenes de 18 a 24 años, encontramos que lo que más preocupa no es la sanidad, sino la vivienda, indicada como el mayor problema por el 35% de los encuestados. El sistema de salud, con 18%, ocupa el tercer lugar, después de la educación que preocupa al 25% de los jóvenes.

En cuánto a los mayores de 65 años, sus preocupaciones principales son las pensiones (para un 30%) y la sanidad. Se sienten más inseguros que los jóvenes, y no están tan preocupados por la educación, que se manifiesta como prioridad para menos del 8 por ciento.

Así que, para concluir, las estadísticas realmente no nos muestran nada: A los jóvenes les preocupa más la educación y encontrar una casa. Los ancianos ponen más énfasis en las pensiones y el sistema de salud. No necesitábamos un sondeo para saberlo.

Listening for detail

3 Students listen again and prioritise the five concerns about society, a) for young people, and b) for senior citizens.

Preparing a presentation

4 Students prepare a presentation on the values of Spanish people, using the points given to structure their work.

Transferring meaning between languages

5a Students translate the sentences into English.

Answers:

1 *What worries Spanish people between the ages of 45 and 54 the most?*

2 *They are the generation that has control and is in charge.*

3 *A lot of them are concerned about education because they have children studying for a degree.*

4 *However, above all they worry about health.*

5 *They are the generation that feels less secure in the street although it is not a terrible worry any longer.*

5b Students translate the sentences into Spanish.

Answers:

1 *¿Qué nos muestran las estadísticas?*

2 *Los jóvenes tienen sus propias preocupaciones y los mayores, las suyas.*

3 *Aquello/Lo que se valora depende de quien se es.*

4 *La supuesta lista de los valores típicos de los españoles no siempre se puede aplicar a todos.*

Strategies for reading authentic texts

6a Students use the strategies given to read the text.

Answers:

5 *Hecho a la medida*

6b Students say whether the statements are true or false.

Answers:

1 *True*

2 *False*

3 *False*

4 *True*

5 *True*

Structuring an argument

7 Students structure an argument for an essay on the subject 'La tecnología da libertad'.

Summarising a text

8 Students write a summary on the text given, making sure to include the following points:

♦ ¿Qué son los art toys?

♦ ¿Qué está pasando en nuestra sociedad?

♦ ¿Por qué no son sorprendentes los art toys?